MBA Swiss Knife

MBA Swiss Knife

Quick Access to Key MBA Concepts

Johnny M. Matta

ISBN-13: 978-1496184221
ISBN-10: 149618422X

For questions or comments, email the author at:
mbaswissknife@gmail.com

To my family.

ACKNOWLEDGMENTS

I would like to thank the Boustany Foundation for funding my MBA studies; without their support I would not have been able to write this book.

Of equal importance for this endeavor were my professors and classmates at Cambridge University who took the time and effort to help me learn and digest the concepts introduced in the MBA curriculum.

I am also grateful to many of my friends and colleagues who have believed in me and encouraged me to complete this project. Special thanks to the many fellow alumni at Stanford and Cambridge who have generously shared their thoughts on various subjects related to writing and publishing this book. I am also happy to acknowledge the help of Ms. Mandi Vartenuk, J.D. for editing my manuscript, and I wish to thank the following people for their feedback and support: Ayşe Alagöz, Charlotte Hamaoui, Eid Eid, Elizabeth H Luna, Hania Chahal, Jean-Jacques Mollo, Jochen Runde, Lee Allen, Moussa Baradhy, Ralph Achkar, Rasha Salman, Sheila Henderson, Tina Hoskin, Yanya Viskovich, and Zeina Mir Ali. Lastly, my love and thanks go to my sisters and my parents who have been supportive of this project from day one.

INTRODUCTION

This book is intended as a quick reference to key concepts found in a typical Master of Business Administration (MBA) program. It has been written with the goal of assisting graduate students enrolled in an MBA program or similar field, as well as MBA holders, by serving as a "cheat sheet" and is not meant to be used as a substitute for the thorough training one receives in business school. The curriculum of a typical MBA program encompasses a number of subjects and disciplines in the field of business and administration in order to give the degree holder the capability to perform a variety of tasks within a firm. This book covers concepts applied in the following areas:

- Economics:
  - Macroeconomics.
  - Microeconomics.

- Corporate Finance:
  - Project decision making.
  - Bonds.
  - Options.
  - Stocks.
  - Hedging.
  - Firm valuation.
  - Capital budgeting.

- Accounting:
  - Balance sheets.
  - Profit and loss statements.
  - Cash flow statements.
  - Indicators of firm performance based on financial statements.

- Strategy:
    - Environment and industry analysis.
    - Competitive analysis.
    - Analysis of the organization with a focus on corporate and business strategies.
    - Combining various strategy frameworks.
    - Tips for strategy consulting work.

- Marketing:
    - Marketing management.
    - Customer relationship management.
    - Product and service line management.
    - Brand management.

- Organizational Behavior:
    - Vision and strategy of the firm.
    - Culture and values.
    - Management and decision making.
    - Human capital management.
    - Organizational change management.

- Operations Management:
    - Transformation processes.
    - Operations planning.
    - Process improvement.
    - Quality control.

- Quantitative Analysis:
    - Probability theory.
    - Modeling.
    - Decision making tools.

Although the chapter titles appear to address only the core subjects of the MBA curriculum, this book covers a substantial part of the concepts, frameworks, theories, and definitions found in a typical MBA program.

SUMMARY OF CONTENTS

DETAILED CONTENTS

MBA Swiss Knife

I. ECONOMICS

"The love of economy is the root of all virtue." – George Bernard Shaw

The area of economics focuses on the mechanisms, decisions, and rules underpinning the investment of labor, resources, and capital required to produce and distribute products and services[1]. The overall economic environment in which these investment and production activities take place is known as the market.

The market is subject to rules set forth by more or less stringent government policies both on the national and international level. In so called free markets, investment, production, and distribution choices of individuals, firms, or countries are virtually unrestricted. Varying levels of restrictions arise in regulated markets, ranging from lightweight and occasional government intervention to strictly planned economies. Given market particularities as well as the limited supply (or scarcity) of labor, natural resources, and other inputs facing any person, group of people, or country, the discipline of economics analyzes and

---

[1] Products and services are collectively referred to as goods.

makes recommendations for the following:

- Investment decisions, particularly as they relate to which goods to produce and introduce (e.g., consumer goods or capital goods[2]).
- Production decisions, mainly in terms of production methods (e.g., using more labor intensive or capital intensive methods, relying on a number of small firms in competition with each other or a few large ones that control the market).
- Distribution, meaning who should have access to the resulting output (e.g., distribution of income, taxation).

Macroeconomics focuses on the study of economics at the aggregate level of countries or regions. Microeconomics is the study of economics at the micro level, with a focus on consumers, households, companies, or specific industries. This chapter will cover:

- Macroeconomics.
- Microeconomics.

Macroeconomics

Macroeconomics takes an aggregate approach and examines the economy as a whole at a regional, national, and global scale. The discussion on macroeconomics covers:

---

[2] Consumer goods are finished products or services that can be purchased and utilized by consumers, whereas capital goods are not meant for consumption but used to produce other goods. A factory is an example of a capital good.

- The overall health of the economy.
- The government's role.

Overall Health of the Economy

The metrics that economists use to assess the health of an economy consist of:

- Gross Domestic Product (GDP).
- Investment levels by the private sector and expenditure amounts by the government.
- Consumption (i.e., expenditure levels) by households.
- Inflation, which impacts variations in the price of goods.
- Unemployment figures and wage levels, which reflect consumers' buying power.
- International trade.

Gross Domestic Product

The Gross Domestic Product (GDP) is the total monetary value of products and services produced within the scope of a country's economic environment. Another macroeconomic indicator is the Gross National Product (GNP), which is similar to the GDP except that it covers both national and international outputs of domestic firms. In other words, the GDP reflects the performance of the local economy of a country, whereas the GNP measures the performance of a country irrespective of geographic boundaries. Today, the GDP is more commonly used than the GNP.

As an overall indicator of the performance of an economy[3], the GDP can be calculated as:

$$GDP = [investments + (government\ spending)] + consumption + (exports - imports)$$

Investments and Government Spending

Investments are key determinants of supply in a given market. Investment levels refer to the amount of resources allocated to purchase the capital goods needed for a given project, with an expectation of making a return. Note that these investments do not include the acquisition of financial instruments such as stocks and bonds. Investors assess the worthiness of investments using cash flow projections and net present value analyses based on the opportunity cost of capital, which is the next best investment return rate with the same level of risk as the chosen investment[4]. If a project is expected to yield a return higher than the prevailing interest rates (in which investors will otherwise invest their resources), the project is deemed worthwhile. As a result, interest rates have a significant impact on investment levels. If rates fall, the cost of investment decreases and a greater number of projects become viable. On the other hand, an increase in interest rates results in a general decrease of capital investments.

---

[3] Overall change in economic activity can be measured by the percentage change in GDP over a period of time such as a year. A decline is referred to as contraction and an increase as growth.

[4] See the chapter on Corporate Finance.

In addition to prevailing interest rates, factors impacting investment levels include consumer spending confidence as reflected by the Consumer Price Index (CPI)[5], labor costs, extent of local and foreign competition, availability of knowledge and technologies, as well as applicable laws and government policies[6].

Consumption

The purchasing activities of consumers is known as consumption, another key determinant of demand in a given market, and is often related to consumers' income.

Some economists claim that present consumption patterns are directly related to current levels of disposable income[7], while others maintain that consumers' present consumption decisions are based on their predictions of their future income levels.

Short and long term tax rates are also believed to influence consumption, particularly due to their direct effect on disposable income levels.

Inflation

Inflation is the increase in the price of goods,

---

[5] CPI is the price of purchasing a set of goods commonly needed by a typical household. Other price indices include the producer price index (PPI) and the GDP deflator.
[6] E.g., research and development subsidies.
[7] Income minus applicable taxes. Note that discretionary income is disposable income minus expenses needed to maintain a certain standard of living.

which results in the decrease of purchasing power. In academic terms, inflation is the percentage rate of the yearly increase in the overall price of products and services, typically measured by the Consumer Price Index (CPI).

Unemployment

Unemployment occurs when individuals willing to work cannot find a job. Unemployment is measured by:

$$(unemployment\ rate) = \frac{(unemployed\ workers)}{(size\ of\ labor\ force)}$$

Unemployment can take various forms including:

- Cyclical unemployment: A result of cyclical increases and decreases in economic activity.
- Frictional unemployment: A consequence of individuals voluntarily abandoning their job[8] or losing their position due to incompatibilities with the role. In these cases, unemployment is usually limited in duration and does not reflect a slowdown in overall business activity[9]. Because some people will always be in between jobs, it is often accepted that some level of unemployment will always exist[10], regardless of market conditions.

---

[8] E.g., to search for a better fit, change fields, or move to another geographical area.

[9] In fact, the willingness of people to voluntarily abandon their job and look for another one may indicate high confidence in the state of the economy.

[10] Aka natural rate of unemployment.

- Structural unemployment: Brought on by changes in production methods, technologies, tastes, etc. For example, the introduction of automobiles led to a decrease in jobs related to horse breeding and carriage assembly, which were replaced by new jobs in the automotive industry, hence those lost jobs created structural unemployment.

Some economists argue that unemployment and inflation are related. The Phillips Curve[11] suggests a negative correlation between inflation and unemployment, meaning that governments may be able to control both. This inverse relation was initially accepted as valid until the 1970s when a number of countries experienced so called stagflation, which results from high levels of both inflation and unemployment. Given that such a situation was not possible based on the Phillips Curve, economists (particularly Milton Friedman), discredited the inverse relation by claiming that it only applied to short term periods and did not pertain to the long term. Today, no single model seems to relate the two parameters on a general scale. Although an overall sense of inverse relation persists, various models are applied to specific scenarios, particularly in terms of short term and long term unemployment prospects.

---

[11] Named after William Phillips' analysis of the link between unemployment and inflation (Phillips, A. W., The Relation between Unemployment and the Rate of Change of Money Wage Rates in the United Kingdom, 1861-1957). Economica, New Series, Vol. 25, No. 100 (Nov., 1958), pp. 283-299.

International Trade

International trade is the exchange of goods (import and export) between countries. Factors and indicators of international trade include:

- The country's comparative advantage.
- The country's balance of payments.
- Exchange rates.

Comparative Advantage

The comparative advantage of a country reflects its ability to produce a product or service at a lower cost than other countries. This production edge can be due to superior labor, know how, weather conditions[12], geographic location, etc. A country should allocate its resources to those areas of specialized production in which it enjoys a comparative edge.

Even if a country has the ability to produce all of its products and services at a lower cost than that of its trading partners[13], that country is still better off limiting its production to the areas where it is most efficient, exporting the product, and importing other goods that it may need. Both the country under consideration and its trading partners will benefit more from this approach than from producing in isolation. The following example clarifies this theory:

Assume country A is more efficient than country B

---

[12] E.g., wine production is favored by certain weather conditions.

[13] A situation known as absolute advantage.

in the production of virtually any good. The two countries both produce computers and shoes and their only input into the production process is labor. Their respective production efficiencies are listed below.

	Time to produce	
Country	1 computer	1 shoe pair
A	10 hours	1 hours
B	50 hours	2 hours

Production efficiency of countries A and B

If each country produces in isolation and allocates half its work force hours to producing computers and the other to producing shoes, the result after say 2,000 hours of work will be as follows:

Country	Computers	Shoe pairs
A	100	1,000
B	20	500
Total	120	1,500

Production output without trade or specialization

If country B specialized its production in shoes and allocated all 2,000 hours to the task and country A spent 30% of available man hours (600 hours) on shoes and the remainder on computers (1,400 hours) and then the two countries traded their products, the result would be:

Country	Computers	Shoe pairs
A	140	600
B	0	1,000
Total	140	1,600

Production output with trade or specialization

The cumulative output is therefore higher for both countries if they specialize.

Balance of Payments

The Balance of Payments (BOP) illustrates the trade performance of a given economy as reflected by the total value of imports versus exports in terms of goods, or financial capital.

Balance of payments are similar to a firm's financial cash flow statements[14] in that they extend over a certain period (e.g., a quarter or a year) and list the monetary value of all trades by domestic entities, whether private or public. A positive BOP indicates a trade surplus, while a negative balance reflects a trade deficit[15].

Governments often adapt their trade policies to boost exports and reduce imports, mainly because more exports yield higher revenues, while fewer imports raise employment.

Exchange Rates

Exchange rates are the value differences of monetary currencies between countries. Such rates can have a significant impact on international trade as they may affect the attractiveness of foreign products, depending on the conversion rate. For example, if a Japanese car manufacturer sells a vehicle at 2 million Yen, and the exchange rate is 100 Yen for 1 US

---

[14] See the chapter on Accounting.
[15] Theoretically, if all credit and debit transactions are recorded, the BOP should equal zero. This is because even in the case of a deficit, the funds to buy imported goods must come from somewhere and if included in the BOP calculation will cancel the deficit value.

Dollar, the cost of buying the Japanese car in the US market will be $20,000 (disregarding shipment costs, tariffs, etc.). Conversely, if the US Dollar appreciates versus the Yen at a rate of 150 to 1, the cost of the same product for an American consumer becomes $13,334.

Exchange rates vary depending on market supply and demand for various monetary currencies. If a central bank offsets the market fluctuation by buying or selling enough of its currency, it will, for the most part, maintain fixed rates. Otherwise, currency rates vary and are said to float.

Government Role

Governments often play a crucial role in the market environments under their jurisdiction and occasionally influence others indirectly (e.g., US government policies impact the US macro economy which itself affects most of the world economy).

Government intervention aims at battling inflation and unemployment as well as avoiding and recovering from recessions[16]. A government's role is defined through:

---

[16] Simply put, recessions occur when consumers and investors are reluctant to spend money due to a fear of uncertain sustained employment or future returns. Recessions can cause increased unemployment, bankruptcies, reduced availability of credit, reduced investment, reduced trade, and reduced consumer spending. Recessions are to be distinguished from depressions, which are severe cases of recession extending over long time periods.

- Government intervention models.
- Fiscal policies.
- Monetary policies.
- Protectionism and trade agreements.

Government Intervention Models

In the days of feudal systems, government interference was used to protect the prerogatives of the ruling caste[17]. With the advent of the industrial revolution and the unprecedented opportunity it brought to entrepreneurs willing to use new production technologies to change the rules of the game, markets started transforming, relying on the balance between the supply and demand. Adam Smith, arguably the first modern economist, advanced his invisible hand theory, which he described as the ability of individuals to balance and create wealth in free markets by investing, producing, and distributing without any government intervention or monopoly rule[18].

However, Smith's theory was challenged as the substantial economic growth brought about by the industrial revolution was also accompanied by difficult labor conditions and questions concerning the distribution of wealth. The first big recession in 1929 also raised doubts about the value of a completely free market, or a *laissez-faire*[19] economy, as advocated by

---

[17] This is referred to as mercantilism.

[18] This also implies strict antitrust laws, meaning that no two or more entities are allowed to collude in any way (e.g., by fixing prices) that will affect the free functioning of supply and demand mechanics in the market.

[19] The French term for "leave it be."

Smith.

John Maynard Keynes[20] suggested a market model that sits somewhere between free and planned markets[21]. His theory asserts that governments should intervene when demand slows down. Such slowdowns may be due to decreased demand by investors and consumers who, for various reasons, become weary of spending their money on goods. As a result, production decreases, affecting wages, unemployment, and further decreases in investment and consumption. To break this vicious cycle, Keynes proposed that governments can stimulate the economy by lowering interest rates, thereby increasing the availability of capital, which individuals and businesses will then spend on goods. The resultant higher demand levels lead to a corresponding rise in supply. Today, most free market economies use some form of Keynesian government intervention.

Lastly, the monetarist theory, introduced by Milton Friedman, opposes Keynes' approach and asserts that economies function best when left alone. Major economic crises have often led to a renewed discussion about the best approach to macroeconomic management[22], and different countries have adopted

---

[20] Keynes, John M., and Paul R. Krugman. *The general theory of employment, interest, and money*. Houndmills, Basingstoke, Hamshire New York, NY: Palgrave Macmillan, 2007. Print.
[21] E.g., the former Soviet Union had a planned market.
[22] E.g., the Great Depression in the 1930s subsequently led to a shift towards interventionism; high unemployment and inflation in the 1970s led to a shift towards monetarist views; and the Black Monday crash of 1987 led to a renewed debate about the prevailing monetarist view.

one or a combination of the two theories. The United States leans more towards Friedman's monetarist view; however, the 2007 recession initiated the emergence of broad government intervention policies.

Fiscal Policies

Fiscal policies attempt to control government taxing, spending, and borrowing in order to regulate market fluctuations. Free market economies may even benefit from some level of this type of government intervention, particularly during recession times, at least according to the Keynesian theory.

By increasing its investment during slow economic periods[23], awarding unemployment benefits, cutting taxes[24], or adjusting trade fees[25], the government can restore consumer and investor confidence just enough to get them spending again, triggering a revitalization in the economy.

When the economy is growing, governments collect taxes on high returns within the private sector, build up reserves, reduce their spending, and pay off their debts. This accumulated wealth can also be tapped in future downturns. The concern with growing economies is inflation, but again, governments can somewhat control the situation using various monetary policies.

---

[23] E.g., by initiating construction or transportation projects.
[24] Tax cutting impacts income levels and investment tax.
[25] E.g., raising custom duties on imports can favor national industries, albeit with the possibility of foreign retaliation which can affect exports.

Monetary Policies

Monetary policies aim to control the supply of credit, or the amount which can be borrowed. This is primarily achieved by setting the interest rate at which individuals and businesses can borrow money.

When the economy is slow, governments lower interest rates. This encourages more people and firms interested in borrowing money to spend and undertake various projects, therefore growing and strengthening the economy. On the other hand, a rapidly swelling economy can result in inflation as rising demand is met with price increases. In this case, governments may raise interest rates in order to bring the situation under some measure of control. Higher interest rates decrease borrowing and spending, which reduces the demand for goods and in turn, regulates inflation.

Protectionism and Trade Agreements

Protectionism policies favor locally produced goods at the expense of foreign ones. A country may impose taxes on foreign products and services (referred to as tariffs), adopt import or export quotas, or prohibit specific imports or exports altogether.

Trade policies take into account import tariffs, the safety of imported goods, maintaining good relations with trade partners, and protecting national production. Governments engage in trade discussions to devise mutually beneficial agreements.

As their name indicates, trade agreements are inter country contracts that regulate taxes, exchange volumes, restrictions, and other elements of the exchange of goods between two or more countries.

Examples include:

- The Asean Free Trade Area (AFTA) (six Southeast Asian countries).
- The European Union (27 European states).
- The Greater Arab Free Trade Area (GAFTA) (14 Arab states).
- The North American Free Trade Agreement (NAFTA) (Canada, Mexico, and the United States).

Microeconomics

While macroeconomics analyzes the economy on a national or global level, microeconomics focuses its analysis on consumers, an organization, or a particular industry. Topics of interest include:

- Models of competition.
- Relationship between supply and demand.
- Analysis of cost versus profit.

Models of Competition

Models of competition are the competitive environments in which firms and individuals compete within the scope of a certain industry.

Under an extreme scenario, an undisputed single seller provides to the whole market and determines prices, thereby creating a pure monopoly.

In a more intense competitive landscape, many sellers will offer similar products with some level of differentiation between them. Each seller will take a small part of the market share and prices will be determined by supply and demand. This is referred to as monopolistic competition as each player has somewhat of a monopoly over his or her own differentiated product.

When a few players dominate the scene and consumers have limited alternatives, the market is said to be an oligopoly. Players in such markets often manage to maintain prices at high levels, although price wars sometimes occur and drive prices down. Governments may enforce anti-trust laws[26] in order to avoid price collusion between sellers.

Lastly, in a near perfect competitive market structure, sellers and buyers are abundant, products are similar and substitutable, and market entry or exit is free. In this case, prices are determined by a perfectly elastic demand curve[27], as the supply is so diversified that an increase in demand will not lead to an increase in price.

Relationship between Supply and Demand

The price of an offering depends on the extent of consumer demand as well as the availability of the same or similar offering (the supply). The production of such an offering also depends on the balance between demand and supply. In other words, both prices and production levels will vary depending on the law of supply and demand.

---

[26] Regulations that ensure a competitive rather than a monopolistic market.
[27] The elastic demand curve is discussed in more detail in the section below.

Changes in Supply and Demand

Supply and demand analyses rely on the supply and demand curves. The former reflects the change in production levels for various price points, while the latter relates consumers' willingness to buy versus the price of goods. If prices increase (decrease) while supply remains constant, demand will go down (up) as less (more) people will be interested in purchasing the goods.

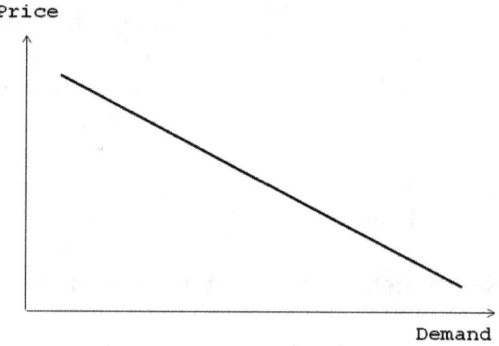

Illustration of a demand curve

Similarly, if prices increase (decrease) while demand remains constant, supply will go up (down) as firms will be interested in producing more (less) firms of these goods.

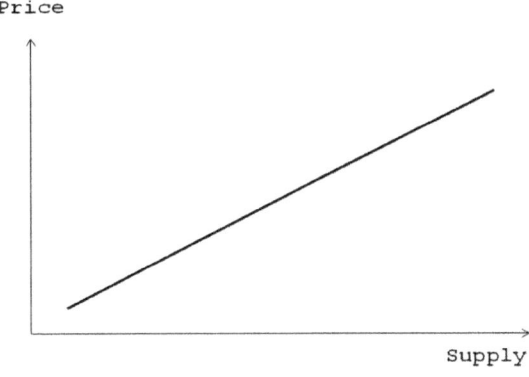

Illustration of a supply curve

In reality, prices, supply, and demand will keep fluctuating until a point of equilibrium is reached.

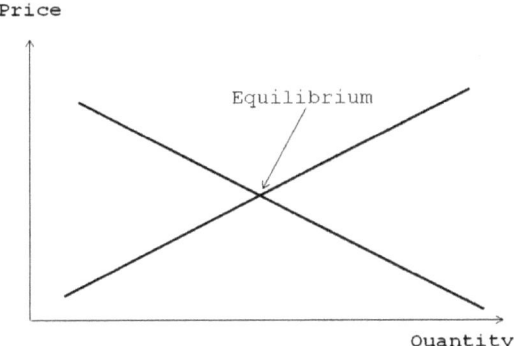

Equilibrium between supply and demand

The relationship between supply and demand can be complicated by such factors as the desire for purchase created by marketing campaigns, inherent scarcity of the offering in question[28], cultural factors, consumer tastes, trends, externalities[29], and others.

Elasticity

Managers are also interested in the so called price elasticity of demand (supply), which is the expected change in demand (supply) for a 1% increase in price. When a change in price will significantly impact demand (supply), it is referred to as elastic demand (supply). If price remains almost constant regardless of demand (supply), then demand (supply) is said to be perfectly elastic.

Perfectly elastic demand occurs under theoretical conditions in which the good under consideration is hard to differentiate[30] (e.g., wheat), and there are an infinite number of suppliers willing to offer the same good at the same price point. Perfectly elastic supply occurs under theoretical conditions in which the producers' cost to offer a good is the same regardless of quantities produced, and there are an infinite number of suppliers willing to offer the same good at the same price point.

---

[28] Scarcity refers to the gap between demand and availability of an offering. Some goods may have a limited supply no matter how much producers try to increase production. For example, strategic land locations, unique art work, or endangered species cannot be duplicated or substituted.

[29] Externalities are side effects of production that may impact price such as pollution or accidents (e.g., nuclear power plant failure or oil spills). Such effects can impact pricing by causing consumer defection, increased regulations, etc.

[30] This is referred to as a commodity item.

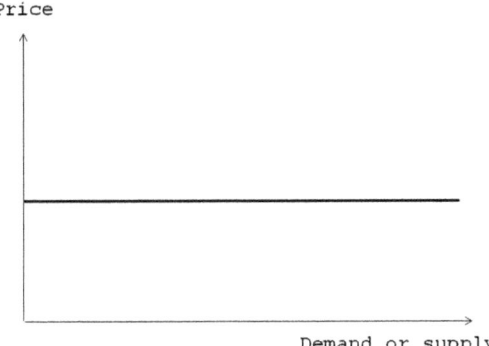

Perfectly elastic demand or supply

When demand (supply) will theoretically be maintained regardless of price, it is said to be perfectly inelastic. Perfectly inelastic demand can occur in the case of non replaceable and essential goods (e.g., water), while perfectly inelastic supply occurs when resources are inherently scarce, and no matter how much they try, producers will not be able to offer more of the goods (e.g., rare minerals).

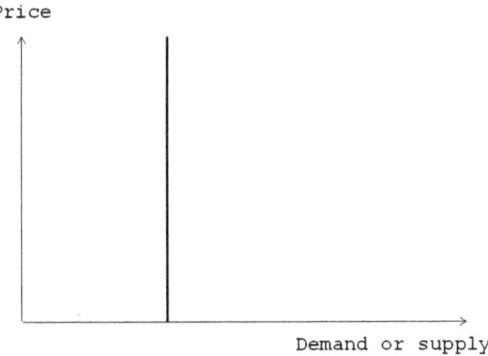

Perfectly inelastic demand or supply

Marginal Utility

Marginal utility reflects a consumer's gain or loss on the purchase of one item of a given product or service. Marginal utility drives consumption patterns because low or negative marginal utility indicates the consumer has little to gain or something to lose by making the purchase. For example, a consumer who is hungry will have a high marginal utility for a sandwich, but once eaten, there will be little to gain from buying a second sandwich and a third sandwich will simply be left to rot.

Consumer and Producer Surpluses

Consumer surplus reflects the gain made by consumers who are able to purchase a good at a price lower than they may be willing to pay. Conversely, producer surplus is the gain that producers make when they are able to sell at a price higher than what they are willing to sell for.

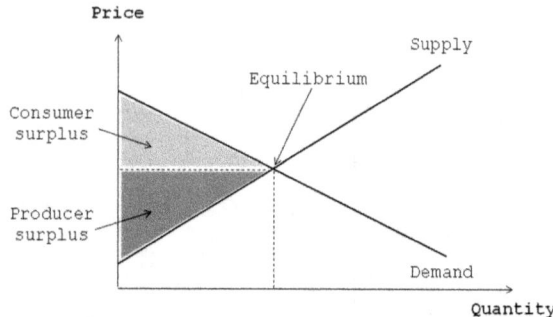

Illustration of consumer and producer surpluses

Analysis of Cost Versus Profit

As described above, prices are a primary factor of supply and demand. Obviously, a firm that launches a good will typically price it so to recoup its cost of production and gain a certain margin[31]. However, if the firm under consideration does not erect strong barriers to entry[32], free market rules dictate that other producers will inevitably start providing similar goods which will lead to an increase in supply. Prices and demand will start varying, as will supply, until an equilibrium price point is reached, which may be different than the launch price of the offering.

As changes in market conditions occur, producers will constantly assess their revenues versus their cost[33]. This is because profits are governed by this simple equation:

$$profits = revenues - costs$$

Firms will also keep an eye on the opportunity cost, which is the use of the same resource for other purposes. Opportunity cost can be measured in terms of both monetary and non-monetary value. An

---

[31] As described in the chapter on Marketing, managers may adopt various pricing strategies that may ignore the underlying cost of production for a certain time in order to build demand. Alternatively, firms may aim for disproportionate margins solely based on the nature of certain goods, such as luxury items, or the strength of the firm's brand name.
[32] Obstacles to prevent other firms from producing the same good. An example is a patent which prevents non authorized replication of intellectual property. See the chapter on Strategy.
[33] Cost can be fixed or variable. The former remains the same, irrespective of output (e.g., rent), while the latter varies with production outputs.

example of the former is the opportunity cost of capital, which is the next best investment return rate with the same level of risk as the chosen investment[34]. Loss of time or benefits in engaging in other activities is also considered an opportunity cost (e.g., choosing to watch television instead of reading a book).

When a firm gains a large market share, its cost of production is expected to decrease as dictated by the experience curve[35]. As a result, competitors may not be able to keep up and stay profitable as prices go down. Technological knowhow may also force some producers to reduce their supply or exit that market altogether. Enter the so called marginal cost of production (MC), which is the change in costs in response to a one unit change in output levels. Similarly, marginal revenue from production (MR) is the change in revenue in response to a one unit change in output levels. As long as the marginal revenue is higher than the marginal cost, firms will benefit from increasing their production levels. As MR and MC converge at the same value, a one unit increase in production output will lead to an equal amount of cost and revenue, rendering the increase useless. As a result, firms set their production levels so that MC equals MR[36].

---

[34] See the chapter on Corporate Finance.
[35] Increasingly relevant as the firm's market share and output levels increase. See the chapter on Strategy.
[36] Assumes perfectly competitive markets which are only approximately achieved in real life. In such markets, firms are "price takers," meaning they have no ability to control prices that are solely determined by supply and demand.

II. CORPORATE FINANCE

"Finance, like time, devours its own children." – Honoré de Balzac

Corporate finance is an essential function of a firm. It can affect many financial aspects of the company's management decisions such as what to invest in, how to finance investments, and how to value stocks and corporations. This chapter will cover:

- Project decision making.
- Bonds.
- Options.
- Stocks.
- Hedging.
- Firm valuation.
- Capital budgeting.

Project Decision Making

Decisions regarding the allocation of resources are at the core of corporate finance. These decisions require an examination of various projects, an estimation of the potential revenues and risks associated with each, followed by a resolution about which endeavors to pursue. The following concepts and tools are essential for project decision making:

- Present value.
- Net present value.
- Internal rate of return (IRR).
- Payback period.
- Profitability index.
- Depreciation.
- Capital asset pricing model.
- Portfolio management.

Present Value Calculation

The present value of cash flow spread over the future represents the current dollar value of the entire stream of future earnings and/or expenditures.

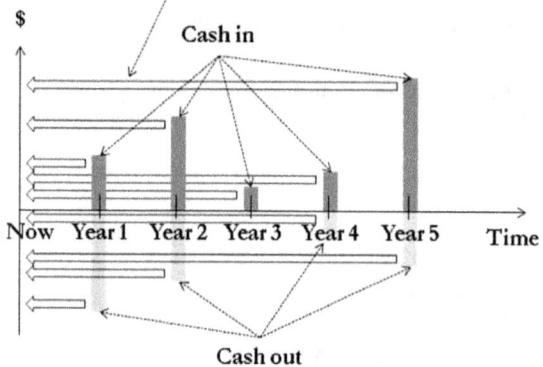

Illustration of cash flow discounting

Present values offer a single dollar figure which can be used to assess the value of a project as well as compare a project's worth with that of others'. In addition, the present value calculation allows financial managers to account for the so called time value of money, which refers to the fact that a dollar today is worth more than a dollar tomorrow as a dollar in hand can be immediately invested to generate interest or profit and because the dollar's value decreases with time due to inflation.

The present value (PV) of a future value (FV) is calculated as follows, with r representing the opportunity cost of capital[37]:

$$PV = \frac{FV}{1+r}$$

When a stream of future cash payments is involved, the present value can be expressed as:

$$PV = \sum_{i=1}^{n} \frac{C_i}{(1+r)^i}$$

Where C_i is the earning and/or expense in period[38] i, r is the opportunity cost of capital, and n is the number of periods. Note that the discount factor for period i is given by:

$$DCF_i = \frac{1}{(1+r)^i}$$

---

[37] Opportunity cost of capital (aka discount rate) is the next best investment return rate with the same level of risk. Note that if the opportunity cost of capital is estimated from historical data, arithmetic averages are more appropriate than the compound annual rates of return (aka geometric average return).

[38] A year, quarter, month, etc.

Real and Nominal Interest Rates

Generally and unless stated otherwise, interest rates and dollar values are stated in nominal terms. Nominal values are not adjusted for inflation, whereas real (aka effective or actual) values are. The interest rate must be adjusted for inflation if all cash flow figures are adjusted. In other words, one must use real interest rates with real cash flows and nominal interest rates with nominal cash flows. The real interest rate can be calculated as follows:

$$(real\ interest\ rate) = \frac{1 + r_{nominal}}{1 + r_{inflation}} - 1$$

As for real cash flow figures, they account for the fact that the purchasing power of money decreases with time due to inflation. If a nominal cash flow is examined i years from today, the corresponding real value in i years can be determined by:

$$(real\ cash\ flow)_{in\ year\ i} = (nominal\ cash\ flow)_{in\ year\ i} \times (1 - r_{inflation})^i$$

As inflation is usually positive, the real interest rate is usually lower than the nominal rate. Of course, the opposite will apply in the case of deflation when the inflation rate is negative. Consider a future payment worth a nominal $100.00 two years from today, while the inflation rate is 2% and the nominal interest rate is 10%. The present value of that future payment can be calculated in two ways, both of which give approximately the same result. Using nominal values:

$$PV = \frac{\$100}{(1 + 10\%)^2} = \$82.64$$

With real values, both the $100.00 and the 10% figure have to be adjusted for inflation as follows:

$$(real\ interest\ rate) = \frac{1 + 10\%}{1 + 2\%} - 1 = 7.84\%$$

$$(\$100)_{real} = \$100 \times (1 - 2\%)^2 = \$96.04$$

As a result, the adjusted present value becomes:

$$PV = \frac{\$96.04}{(1 + 7.84\%)^2} = \$82.57$$

Present Value Formulae

The following formulae calculate the present value of a stream of yearly cash payments C with an interest rate r. Perpetuity means the payments never end, a t-period annuity means payments end after t years, a growing annuity means yearly payments grow at a steady rate, and continuously compounded interest is calculated continuously as opposed to compounding at regular periods:

Perpetuity:

$$PV = \frac{C}{r}$$

t-period annuity:

$$PV = \frac{C}{r} \times \left(1 - \frac{1}{(1 + r)^t}\right)$$

Growing annuity:

$$PV = \frac{C}{r - g}$$

t-period annuity growing at rate g:

$$PV = \frac{C}{r - g} \times [1 - \frac{(1 + g)^t}{(1 + r)^t}]$$

Continuously compounded interest:

$$PV = C \times e^{-rt}$$

t-period annuity with compounded interest:

$$PV = \frac{C}{r} \times (1 - e^{-rt})$$

Net Present Value Calculation

Net Present Value (NPV) calculation combines initial investments with future expenses and returns (at the current dollar value):

$$NPV = (PV \text{ of future cash flow}) + (immediate\ investment)$$

In corporate finance, the decision to adopt a project starts with calculating the corresponding NPV then moving forward only if:

- $NPV > 0$, and
- NPV is significant enough to make the project worthwhile given any foreseeable risks associated with the venture.

The investment figures in NPV calculations must

be limited to those costs directly related to the project under consideration. Expenditures that were made prior to examining the option to undertake the project and that can no longer be recovered[39] must be excluded from the NPV calculation.

In the 3 year NPV analysis below, a $300,000 initial one time investment is included only because it pertains to the purchase of plant equipment needed to begin production. If the firm had hired a consultant at the rate of $45,000 to perform a feasibility analysis, that cost would not be included in the NPV given that it has already been incurred whether the firm goes ahead with the project or not. In other words, the consultant's fee is a sunk cost. In the same NPV analysis, the values for COGS (Cost of Goods Sold[40]) correspond to variable costs that are incurred by the firm during production.

The fixed plant equipment cost is listed under operating expenses, and it is the only cost that is depreciated at an equal yearly amount (in the calculation, we assume that by the end of the third period the salvage cost of plant equipment is zero, i.e., the cost at which it could be sold is zero[41]). The cost of raw material is not amortized[42] as it is consumed in the production process.

––––––––––––––––––––

[39] Such expenses are referred to as sunk costs.
[40] See the chapter on Accounting.
[41] Otherwise, the salvage cost would have resulted in a taxable positive cash flow in year 3 under plant equipment.
[42] See the chapter on Accounting.

	Year	1	2	3
(in '000)	Sales	$411	$420	$428
A	**Total revenue**	**$411**	**$420**	**$428**
	COGS			
B	Raw material	$41	$42	$43
C	Labor	$62	$63	$64
D=B+C	**Total**	**$103**	**$105**	**$107**
	Operating costs			
E	Plant equipment	$300	$0	$0
F	General Admin	$62	$63	$64
G	Marketing	$82	$84	$86
H	Operations	$37	$38	$39
I=E+F+G+H	**Total**	**$481**	**$185**	**$188**
J=A–D–I	**EBITDA**	-$173	$130	$133
K=D*5%	Interest[43]	$5.14	$5.24	$5.35
L	Depreciation	$100	$100	$100
M=J–K–L	**EBT**	-$078	$25	$27
N=M*30%	Taxes[44]	$0	$7	$8
O=M–N+L	**Net profit**	**-$178**	**$117**	**$119**
1/(1+5%)^{year}	DCF[45]	0.95	0.90	0.86
	PV	-$169	$106	$103
	NPV	**$40**		

Example of a 3 years NPV calculation

Note that the NPV value is a positive estimated gain of $40,000. Depending on the risks associated with the venture and other options available to the firm, managers should look favorably at undertaking

---

[43] Assumes COGS are financed by loans at 5% interest rate.
[44] No taxes are paid if Earnings Before Taxes (EBT), which is the taxable revenue, is zero or negative. Assume negative taxes cannot be rolled over to subsequent years, and a 30% flat tax rate.
[45] At 5% opportunity cost of capital.

this initiative.

Internal Rate of Return

Another method used to assess project attractiveness is the Internal Rate of Return (IRR). IRR is the discount rate that sets NPV to zero[46]. Managers should move forward with the project if:

$$IRR > \textit{(opportunity cost of capital)}$$

To determine the IRR for the NPV calculation above, the discount rate that will yield a value of zero for the NPV must be uncovered. Remember that the discount factor (DCF) for year i is calculated as:

$$DCF_i = \frac{1}{(1+r)^i}$$

Microsoft Excel's solver feature calculates the rate at $IRR=21\%$. As 21% is larger than 5%, the IRR method also recommends moving forward with the project.

Payback Period

The payback period can also be used to determine whether a project is worth undertaking as it estimates the time needed to recover the initial investment. To calculate the payback period, the net profits of each year are added until the sum becomes positive, thereby

---

[46] If the project length is one year, the NPV and IRR methods generate the same result; otherwise they may not. The NPV method is generally considered more reliable.

indicating the number of years until the investment is recovered. In the project described above, the calculation would be:

Year	Cumulative sum of net profits
1	-$178,000
2	-$178,000 + $117,000 = -$61,000
3	-$178,000 + $117,000 + $119,000 = +$58,000

Payback period calculation for the project example

It will take three years for the cumulative sum to become positive, hence the payback period is three years.

As can be seen from the calculation, the payback period method does not take the time value of money into consideration because it does not discount future cash flows at the opportunity cost of capital. As such, this method is only to be used as a rough indicator of project attractiveness in combination with NPV or IRR calculations.

Profitability Index

The profitability index (PI) is another rough indicator of project payoff. The index is calculated as follows, with PV_i representing the present value of the cash balance in year i:

$$PI = \frac{\sum_{i=1}^{n} PV_i}{(initial\ investment)}$$

PI values indicate the attractiveness of a project as follows:

- If PI>1, managers should look favorably upon the project because the sum of future cash flows will be higher than the initial investment.
- If PI<1, managers should reject the project.

Returning to the example above, the PI will be[47]:

$$PI = \frac{-\$169k + 106k + \$103k + \$300k}{\$300k}$$
$$= 1.13$$

Again, the recommendation is to go ahead with the project as PI=1.13>1.

Depreciation

The NPV calculation often calls for an estimation of depreciation[48]. Although not cash expenditures in themselves, depreciation amounts are tax deductible in each year they apply, hence their relevance in calculating the NPV after taxes[49].

---

[47] Note that $300,000 has been added to the sum in the numerator as the investment expense is not to be included in the sum of cash flows.

[48] Depreciation and amortization reflect consumption. Both reduce the firm's taxable revenue but are not a cash liability; they simply reflect a decrease in asset value. Depreciation of monetary assets and intangibles is referred to as amortization. Purchased or internally produced assets that are subject to depreciation are referred to as capitalized items (also see the chapter on Accounting).

[49] In accounting, depreciation is significant in that it reflects the loss of an asset's value over time and the corresponding impact on the firm's assets.

Depreciation spreads the cost of capital expenditures over time. If machinery is purchased for $1m and is used over a five year period, depreciation will allocate portions of that $1m to each year of use. This approach will make it appear as if the firm made yearly purchases of equipment, allowing it to take a tax deduction for each of the five years. There are several ways to allocate depreciation amounts over time, three of which are described below:

- Straight line depreciation.
- Declining balance depreciation.
- Sum-of-years-digits depreciation.

Straight Line Depreciation

Straight line depreciation is the simplest and most commonly used method. It calculates the difference between purchase and salvage cost (i.e., price at which the item can be ultimately sold), divided by the number of years under consideration; the result is the depreciation amount allocated to each project year:

$$(yearly\ depreciation\ amount) = \frac{[(purchase\ cost) - (salvage\ cost)]}{(project\ years)}$$

If the purchase cost is $1,000 and the salvage value is $200.00, the yearly depreciation amount for a five year project will be:

$$(yearly\ depreciation\ amount) = \frac{[(\$1,000) - (\$200)]}{(5)} = \$160$$

Year	Start value	Depreciation	End value
1	$1,000	$160	$840
2	$840	$160	$680
3	$680	$160	$520
4	$520	$160	$360
5	$360	$160	$200

Example of straight line depreciation

Declining Balance Depreciation

In the declining balance depreciation approach, the asset is depreciated by the same depreciation rate every year, calculated as follows:

$$(depreciation\ rate) = 1 - [\frac{(salvage\ value)}{(purchase\ cost)}]^{\frac{1}{years}}$$

If the purchase cost is $1,000 and the salvage value is $200.00, the depreciation rate for a five year project will be:

$$(depreciation\ rate) = 1 - [\frac{(\$200)}{(\$1,000)}]^{\frac{1}{5}} = 27.52\%$$

Year	Start value	Depreciation	End value
1	$1,000	$275	$725
2	$725	$199	$525
3	$525	$145	$381
4	$381	$105	$276
5	$276	$76	$200

Example of declining balance depreciation

Sum-of-years-digits Depreciation

As illustrated in the comparison graph below, the

sum-of-years-digits (SOYD) approach most often results in a faster depreciation rate than the straight line or declining balance methods. This means that larger amounts will be depreciated early in the asset's lifetime, therefore allowing for higher tax deductions at the beginning of the project.

The first step of this method is to calculate the sum from 1 to the lifetime of the asset. In other words, if the project is scheduled to last five years, the sum will be:

$$1 + 2 + 3 + 4 + 5 = 15$$

Next, the difference between purchase cost and salvage value is calculated and allocated in annual depreciation amounts as proportions of that difference as follows:

Year	Depreciation
1	$\frac{5}{15} \times [(purchase\ cost) - (salvage\ value)]$
2	$\frac{4}{15} \times [(purchase\ cost) - (salvage\ value)]$
3	$\frac{3}{15} \times [(purchase\ cost) - (salvage\ value)]$
4	$\frac{2}{15} \times [(purchase\ cost) - (salvage\ value)]$
5	$\frac{1}{15} \times [(purchase\ cost) - (salvage\ value)]$

Yearly depreciation amounts with the sum-of-years-digits method

Returning to the earlier example, the depreciation for the five year project will be as follows:

Year	Start value	Depreciation	End value
1	$1,000	$267	$733
2	$733	$213	$520
3	$520	$160	$360
4	$360	$107	$253
5	$253	$53	$200

Example of a sum-of-years-digits depreciation

Note that other depreciation methods do exist[50], some of which vary annual write-off amounts from the asset's value based on actual usage (e.g., miles driven by a vehicle, or number of hours a machine is used).

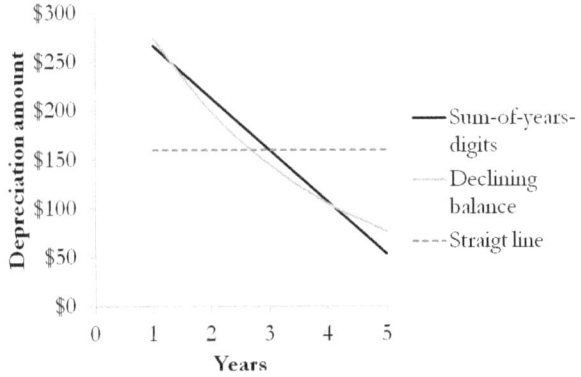

Comparison of depreciation methods

The Capital Asset Pricing Model (CAPM)

The NPV calculations discussed above incorporate a discount rate r or an opportunity cost of capital.

---

[50] E.g., unit-of-production depreciation and hours-of-service depreciation.

Such rates can be projected using the Capital Asset Pricing Model (CAPM). The CAPM estimates the rate of return of a financial security based on general market risk and the security's sensitivity to market movements. The rate of return of a security i is:

$$r_i = r_f + \beta_i \times (r_m - r_f)$$

Where r_f is the risk free rate - generally that of U.S. Treasury bonds[51], $(r_m - r_f)$ is the market risk premium, and β captures stock sensitivity to market movements:

- When $\beta < 0$: The stock moves against the market.
- When $\beta > 1$: The stock moves like the market and amplifies it.
- When $0 < \beta < 1$: The stock moves like the market but not with as much amplitude.
- $\beta m = 1$ (market's beta).
- $\beta_f = 0$ (risk free beta).

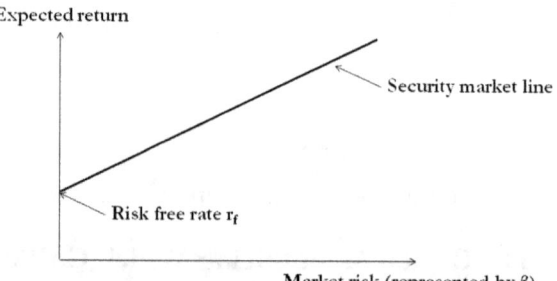

Illustration of return versus market risk

Portfolio Management

Once they calculate project expected NPV values, managers have to choose where to invest. This is referred to as portfolio management and is based on project revenue predictions as well as perceived risks[52].

Portfolio Risk and Return

Just like with any financial security[53], a portfolio presents an expected return, as well as a perceived risk.

The return of a portfolio p is defined by:

$$r_p = \sum_{i=1}^{n} x_i \times r_i$$

Where n is the number of securities in the portfolio and x_i is the proportion invested in portfolio i.

The risk σ_p of portfolio p is defined by:

$$\sigma_p = \sum_{i=1}^{n} \sum_{j=1}^{n} (x_i \times x_j \times \sigma_{i,j})$$

Where n is the number of securities in the portfolio, x_i is the proportion invested in portfolio i, and $\rho_{i,j}$ is the correlation coefficient between securities i and j:

---

[52] See the chapter on Strategy.
[53] Tradable financial instruments such as stocks, options, derivatives, etc.

$$\sigma_{i,j} = \rho_{i,j} \times \sigma_i \times \sigma_j$$

Sensitivity to market movements of the portfolio p is defined by:

$$\beta_p = \frac{\sum_{i=1}^{n} (x_i \times \beta_i)}{n}$$

Where n is the number of securities in the portfolio, x_i is the proportion invested in portfolio i, and:

$$\beta_i = \frac{\sigma_{i,m}}{\sigma_m^2} = \frac{\rho_{i.m} \times \sigma_i \times \sigma_m}{\sigma_m^2}$$

Finally, the portfolio's so called Sharpe ratio[54] is:

$$(Sharpe\ ratio) = \frac{r_p - r_f}{\sigma_p}$$

Portfolio with Borrowing or Lending

Investors may choose to buy a market portfolio A and lend an amount of risk free securities equal to x% of that portfolio. In this case, the resulting portfolio's p return will be defined by:

---

[54] Illustrates the extent to which the portfolio rewards the investor versus the risk. A ratio of 1 or better is considered good, 2 and better is very good, and 3 and better is considered excellent. The Sharpe ratio can also be used to compare two or more portfolios.

$$r_p = (1 + x) \times r_A + x \times r_f$$

And the risk:

$$\sigma_p = (1 - x) \times \sigma_A$$

If the investor buys a market portfolio A, and borrows to buy an additional quantity of that portfolio corresponding to x% of the initial investment, the resulting portfolio's p return will be defined by:

$$r_p = (1 + x) \times r_A - x \times r_f$$

And the risk:

$$\sigma_p = (1 + x) \times \sigma_A$$

The Efficient Frontier

Given a certain amount of cash with which to invest, investors can create a large array of portfolios by allocating various proportions of their wealth to different individual assets available on the market. If all such combinations are plotted in terms of risk versus return, the efficient frontier is the collection of portfolios which yield the maximum return for a given risk. A portfolio is inefficient if there is an alternative with a larger or equal return and lower risk. Note that the market portfolio consists of an investment in every security in the market, with a proportion equivalent to the availability[55] of each[56]. Investors will obviously choose a portfolio that yields the highest return for a given risk, one that lies on the efficient frontier.

The efficient frontier

The leveraged zone is where investors purchase the portfolio with their money and borrow more money to purchase additional portions of the same portfolio. The unleveraged zone is where investors use part of

---

[55] The weight for each security is the ratio of its market value to the sum of the market values of all securities available in the market.

[56] Well diversified portfolios do not involve unique risks (those inherent to a security and that can be eliminated via diversification), only market risk. In other words, the risk of a well diversified portfolio depends on the market risk of the securities included in that portfolio. Diversification can remove unique risk (aka idiosyncratic, unsystematic risk) but cannot remove market risk (aka systematic risk, non-diversifiable risk).

their wealth to purchase the portfolio and another part to lend money at the risk free rate (e.g., US Treasury bonds). The efficient frontier curve is more pronounced in the unleveraged zone as the rate of borrowing money (i.e., leveraged investment) is usually higher than the rate of lending money (i.e., unleveraged investment). The benefit of diversification by investing in a portfolio of individual securities varies with the degree of correlation between the constituting securities in the portfolio. For example, with only two securities (1) and (2) in a given portfolio:

- If $\rho_{1,2}=+1$, there is no benefit from diversification.
- If $\rho_{1,2}=0$, there may be some benefit from diversification.
- If $\rho_{1,2}=-1$, there will be maximum benefit from diversification.

With a correlation $\varrho_{1,2}$ equal to 1, the risk of the portfolio will simply be a weighted average of the underlying securities' risks. For all other values of $\varrho_{1,2}$, the risk will be lower than the weighted average of risks and diversification therefore pays off.

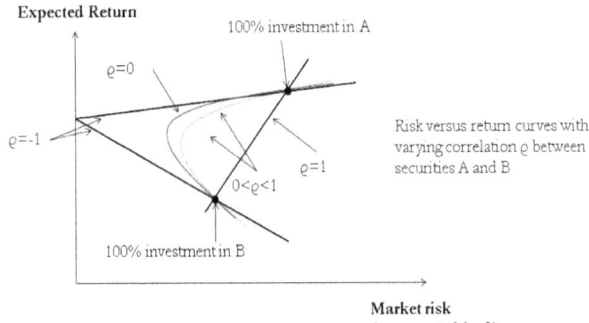

Expected Return

100% investment in A

$\varrho=0$

$\varrho=-1$

$\varrho=1$

$0<\varrho<1$

100% investment in B

Risk versus return curves with varying correlation ϱ between securities A and B

Market risk
(represented by β)

Return versus risk of a portfolio of two securities

On each risk versus return curve[57] movement along the curve occurs with varying investment proportions in each security. The degree of curvature of the curve reflects the correlation coefficient of the two securities.

Bonds

Bonds are debt obligations of the issuer to the holder. The holder buys the bond with the promise of being paid back in the future, either through a combination of regular payments (aka coupons) and a final payment (aka face value) or one final payment[58,59]. Bonds therefore constitute a way for bond issuers to obtain loans from the market.

Bond types vary depending on characteristics that relate to purchase and sale terms, currencies, home country of issuing party, and financial reputation of the issuing party. The following subsections discuss:

- Bond pricing.
- Bond duration.
- Bond volatility.

Bond Pricing

Bond prices reflect the present value of the

---

[57] Not to be confused with the efficient frontier curve as this case examines the portfolio combination of two securities only.
[58] Bonds with no coupon payments are commonly referred to as stripped bonds.
[59] Note that the coupon rate is the value of the regular payment amount divided by that of the final payment.

projected future cash flow for the bond holder:

$$(bond\ price) = \frac{C}{r} \times [1 + \frac{1}{(1+r)^n}] + \frac{FV}{(1+r)^n}$$

Where C is the yearly coupon, FV is the final value, and n is the maturity term (e.g., five years).

YTM (yield to maturity) is the rate at which the above price equation holds, i.e., the interest rate at which the discounted sum of future payments of coupons and final face value will equal today's price of the bond.

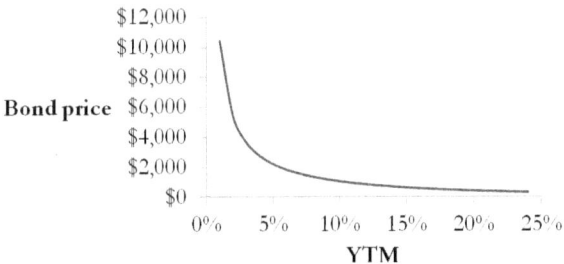

Bond price vs. YTM[60]

- When interest rates go down, bond prices go up and vice-versa. But changes in interest rates impact long term bonds more than short term bonds[61].

---

[60] Bond is characterized by ten years to maturity, $50.00 coupons, and $1,000 face value at maturity.
[61] The reason is because long term bonds will have more payments in the future than short term bonds. The discounting effect of interest rates will therefore bear a greater impact.

- When YTM<(coupon rate), then (bond price)>FV (and vice-versa).

Bond Duration

Bond duration is the weighted average recovery time of the bond's purchase price. Duration is higher when coupon rates are lower, as the bulk of bond payments will be recovered towards maturity. For a bond with n coupons:

$$duration = \sum_{i=1}^{n} i \times \frac{PV(C_i)}{(bond\ price)} + n \times \frac{PV(FV)}{(bond\ price)}$$

Bond Volatility

Bond volatility is the percentage change in bond price as a result of a 1% change in YTM:

$$(bond\ volatility\%) = \frac{duration}{1 + YTM}$$

A higher risk of default by the bond issuer translates into a higher interest rate. The risk of default is available from reputable credit rating agencies[62] which examine the credit worthiness of bond issuers and categorize their bonds. Category names vary depending on the credit agency, but the information all relates to the extent to which a given bond issuer can be trusted to honor the terms of the bonds issued.

---

[62] Moody's, Fitch, and S&P being the most prominent ones.

Options

An option is an investment in a right or capability to carry out an action in the future. There is no obligation to exercise the option, and the holder will only do so if the conditions become favorable[63]. The more uncertainty there is, the more valuable options become. Note that the option holder is not entitled to dividends. The following sub-categories are discussed below:

- Call options.
- Put options.
- Option valuation.
- Futures and forwards.

Call Options

A call option gives its owner the right to buy a stock at a specified exercise or strike price on or before a specified date. Say an investor purchases a call option relating to the price of a given publicly traded stock, and the option has a strike price of $50.00. Further assume the investor pays a price P for that option. The investor is said to be in a long call position as s/he owns the security. The investor has the right to buy the stock at $50.00 (or not buy, at her or his own discretion[64]), a right s/he obviously will not exercise unless the stock price goes above the

---

[63] Exercise terms vary depending on the conditions of the option agreement.
[64] While the investor has the right to exercise her or his option to buy, once s/he does, the seller of the option will have the obligation to sell.

$50.00 strike price, as the stock can be purchased at $50.00 using the option and sold on the market at the higher price. In terms of net profit however, there will be none unless the share's price goes above the strike price by at least the price P of the option. An additional increase in the share price will lead to added profits, which have the potential to skyrocket.

In contrast, the party who sold that option to the investor will be in a short call position as s/he does not own the security. From the point of view of the option's seller, the profit will be P, as long as the share's price remains below the strike price. The moment that changes, net profit starts going down and can potentially translate into a pronounced loss. This begs the question as to why anyone would consider selling such an option. The answer is that sellers of this type of security are usually large banks with large transaction volumes that eventually even each other out while generating revenue from transaction fees.

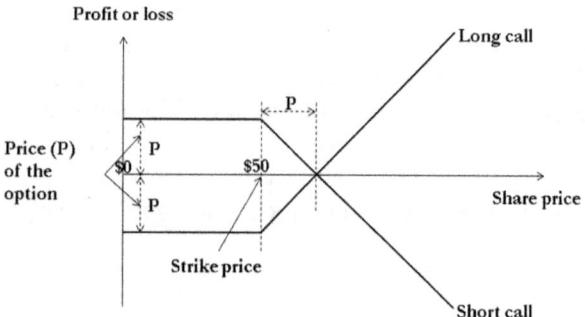

Value of a call option versus share price

Put Options

A put option gives its owner the right to sell stock

at a specified exercise or strike price on or before a specified date.

Say the investor from above purchases a put option with a strike price of $50.00 and pays a price P for that option. Again, assume the option is over the price of a publicly traded stock. The investor is in a long put position as s/he owns a put option security. S/he has the right to sell the stock at $50.00 (or to not sell, at her or his own discretion[65]), a right s/he obviously will not exercise unless the stock price is below the $50.00 strike price, as s/he can then purchase the stock from the market at the lower price and sell it at $50.00 using the option.

In terms of net profit however, there will be none unless the share's price is at least lower than the strike price by the price P of the option. Otherwise, the loss will be capped at P as the investor will simply not exercise the option when the share's price goes above the strike price.

In contrast, the party who sold that option will be in a short put position. From the point of view of the option's seller, the profit will be P, as long as the share's price remains above the strike price. The moment that changes, net profit starts going down and can reach a maximum equal to the value of the strike price.

---

[65] Again, while the investor has the right to exercise her or his option to sell, once s/he does, the seller of the option will have the obligation to buy.

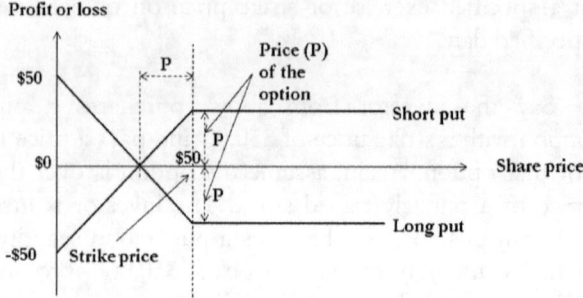

Value of a put option versus share price

Option Valuation

Option price varies with parameters, such as price of the underlying security, exercise price, interest rate, and time to maturity. Assuming the underlying security is stock price (SP), option price:

- Increases as SP increases if the exercise price is constant.
- Decreases when the exercise price increases.
- Increases with both the rate of interest and the time to maturity.
- Increases with both the volatility of the share price and the time to maturity.
- Decreases with increasing exercise price.
- Is higher if written on volatile assets than if written on safe assets.

Option price is defined as:

(option price) = (expected value gained if exercised)
× (probability of exercising)

An option is always riskier than the underlying stock as it has a higher β and a higher σ. Also, the option's risk changes every time the stock price changes. Finally, the higher the stock price versus the exercise price, the safer the call option, although it is always riskier than the stock.

Futures and Forwards

Futures and forwards are future commitments to buy or sell a security; they are not options. Investors can go long or short on futures and forwards.

Futures are obligations like forwards but are standardized by the Stock Exchange. Futures are therefore more liquid[66] than forwards. With forwards, buyers and sellers set their own terms.

Consider the case in which an investor buys a future contract specifying s/he will buy a stock at $50.00. This investor is in a long future position. As long as the price of the stock is below $50.00, the investor will have a negative net profit as honoring her or his obligation to buy at $50.00 means s/he will buy at a price higher than the market rate for the stock under consideration. However, when the stock price exceeds $50.00, the future will become profitable as s/he can buy the stock at $50.00 from the party who sold the future contract and sell on the market at a higher price and make a profit. In the case of this investor, the maximum loss would be $50.00 (because the stock price cannot go below $0), and the maximum profit is virtually unbounded.

---

[66] A liquid asset is considered to be almost equivalent to cash.

In contrast, the party selling the future contract will be in a short future position and will make a maximum of $50.00 if the stock price hits $0, as it will be possible to get that price for free (theoretically), and sell it at $50.00. The loss, however, can be unlimited as the stock price increases.

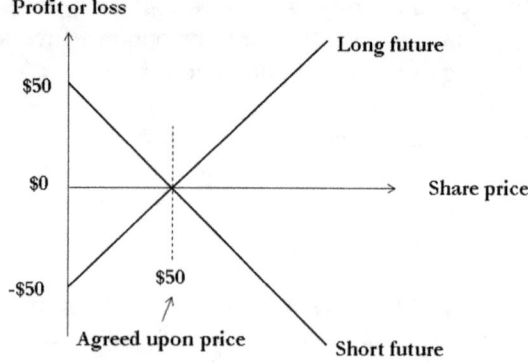

Future contract to buy a stock at $50

Stocks

A corporation is owned by its stockholders (aka shareholders). Firms issue stocks (or shares) to raise equity capital[67] (in order to finance internal projects for example). By purchasing such shares, investors gain participation in the firm's ownership (proportional to the number of stocks they hold versus the total number of issued stocks), and they may also get the right to vote as well as receive

---

[67] One of the limits on the number of shares a firm can issue is the so called authorized capital, which is the maximum number of shares that a firm can issue without the approval of its existing shareholders.

dividend payments when made by the firm. Shares owned by investors are said to be issued and outstanding.

Shares purchased directly from the issuing firm are said to be bought on the primary market. Shares which have been issued and subsequently traded between investors are said to be on the secondary market. Shares traded on the secondary market no longer bring any capital to the issuing firm.

The following subsections will discuss:

- Stock prices.
- Dividends and payout policy.
- Voting for board directors.

Stock Prices

Investor confidence is represented in the firm's market capitalization, which is the total value of issued shares for a publicly traded company[68], as well stock price to earnings (P/E) ratio:

$$(firm\ market\ capitalization) = (\#\ shares) \times SP$$

Where SP is share price.

$$P\!\!\diagup\!\!E = \frac{1}{r_E} = \frac{SP}{EPS}$$

---

[68] Also known as shareholders' equity.

Where r_E is return on equity[69], and EPS is earnings per share.

Also:

$$r_E = \frac{(profit\ after\ tax\ and\ interest) \times (payout\ ratio)}{(firm\ value)}$$

Where the payout ratio is the fraction of net earnings paid to shareholders as dividends.

The price of a share can be calculated as the present value of all future dividend payments. For example, SP of a stock that will have value P_n in year n, and will pay a dividend Div_i for year i is:

$$SP = \sum_{i=1}^{n} \frac{Div_i}{(1+r)^i} + \frac{P_n}{(1+r)^n}$$

If dividends are perpetual and growing at rate g, then SP of the stock is:

$$SP = \frac{Div_1}{(r-g)}$$

Where r is the expected return rate on investment.

---

[69] r_E is the rate of return on common stock. It is the rate that investors can obtain by investing somewhere else (approximations thereof can be obtained by looking at returns for securities with similar risks on the market).

Dividends and Payout Policy

A dividend is a period cash payment given to shareholders by the firm. A dividend payout of 65%, for example, means that for each $1.00 income, the firm sets aside $0.65 as dividends and $0.35 as capital gains.

Dividend payments are determined by a firm's management and depend on the availability of funds in retained earnings, i.e., net profit after all expenses including taxes, as well as a tradeoff analysis between reinvesting the funds[70] and distributing them to shareholders[71]. Firms may also repurchase shares from investors (instead of making a cash dividend payment). Those repurchased shares are held in the company's treasury and are said to remain issued but not outstanding. They are kept in treasury until they are cancelled or resold. Shareholders, therefore, make equity income either through dividends or capital gains on shares they resell on the secondary market (to the issuing firm or other investors).

The payout policy pertains to the manner in which firms decide to pay shareholders from retained earnings. Companies can return cash (payout) to shareholders by:

- Paying them dividends, an action which usually

---

[70] Companies invest in long term assets (property, plant, and equipment) and net working capital.
[71] Note that lenders have first right of claim to cash flow. The stockholder receives whatever cash is left over after the lenders have been paid.

triggers an increase in stock price as the market will perceive that managers will not payout dividends if the company is not healthy.

- Buying back stock, which can happen when the company has excess cash and often leads to an increase in stock price. Stock buyback can change the capital structure[72] by replacing equity with debt (this can be a way to increase debt).

Voting for Board Directors

Stockholders delegate a firm's management decisions to the board of directors, who appoint senior management, who in turn appoint day-to-day managers. Stockholders therefore vote to elect directors, with one share typically representing one vote.

A company can also create different categories of shares (e.g., type A and type B) which receive the same dividends but carry different voting numbers, e.g., a B share has ten votes, while A carries one vote. Obviously, B will be more expensive than A.

Directors are voted upon separately, and shareholders can cast one vote for each share they own. For example, in an election for five vacant director positions, a shareholder with ten shares can cast one vote per vacant seat. If cumulative voting is allowed, the shareholder can cast all votes for one

---

[72] The mix of a firm's debt and equity. Capital structure indicates how the firm is financing its operations; equity comes from investors who buy stakes in the company; and debt consists of loans from banks, bonds, etc.

director.

Finally, it is worth noting that the law in the US and Canada (as well as several other countries) protects minority shareholders (e.g., in the case of oppression by a majority, whereby "unreasonable" decisions are made that go against the clear interests of the minority).

Hedging

Hedging mitigates the risk of a certain investment position by establishing a baseline, i.e., a worst case scenario. To hedge, an investor should purchase securities opposite of the position s/he is in. Hedging is a diversification strategy that relies on the strong negative correlation between two or more positions that an investor adopts (e.g., disaster in a factory investment hedged with insurance will result in a loss of the first but a partial or complete recovery of funds through the insurance policy).

Hedging can apply to a variety of fields including financial investments (e.g., if an investor holds a short option, hedging will translate into purchasing long options), commodities (e.g., airlines buy options on fuel prices to mitigate the possibility of changes in such prices on the market), or currencies (e.g., the purchase of options on foreign currencies to protect against fluctuations in exchange rates).

Hedge Funds

Hedge funds are managed by investment firms that

make investments on behalf of select clients. Investment growth strategy uses shorting and derivatives[73].

Hedge funds charge high performance fees and a minimum fee otherwise. Practically speaking, hedge fund managers buy stock they believe is undervalued, and sell stock deemed to be overvalued, usually from two companies in the same field. As a result, hedge fund managers bet on their expertise, not the market itself (e.g., hedge on Google and Microsoft stocks betting that one of them, based on analysis, will score points over the other due to a new technology, product, etc.).

Firm Valuation

A firm's value V is the sum of its equity E and debt D:

$$V = E + D$$

Estimation of firm value varies with the chosen valuation method. The next section examines:

- The weighted average cost of capital (WACC).
- Valuation methods.

---

[73] Derivatives are financial instruments stemming from something else (e.g., a contract where one party sells a number of stocks in the market at a defined time in the future). The seller's and buyer's loss or gain depends on the future price change of that stock.

Weighted Average Cost of Capital (WACC)

The company weighted average cost of capital (WACC) is a discount rate that can be used to estimate firm or project value by discounting projected cash flows and calculating the present value.

The firm's WACC can only be used for analyzing projects that:

- Are identical in terms of leverage ratio[74] D/V to the firm undertaking them.
- Do not lead to an increase or decrease in the company's overall risk or debt ratios.
- Are not riskier or safer than the average of the firm's existing initiatives.

There are two ways to look at WACC. The first one ignores taxes, in which case:

$$WACC = r_A = \frac{D}{D + E} \times r_D + \frac{E}{D + E} \times r_E$$

Where r_A is the return on a portfolio of all the firm's securities, r_D is the debt interest rate, r_E is the return on equity[75], D is debt, and E is equity. Also:

- $r_E = r_f + \beta_E \times (r_m - r_f)$
- $r_D = r_f + \beta_D \times (r_m - r_f)$
- $r_A = r_f + \beta_A \times (r_m - r_f)$

---

[74] Aka gearing ratio.
[75] The difference between r_E and r_D is that equity holders are residual, meaning they get what is left after interest and debt have been paid.

- $\beta_A = \beta_D \times D/V + \beta_E \times E/V$
- $\beta_E = \beta_A + (\beta_A - \beta_D) \times D/E$

The second way to calculate WACC takes interest tax deductions into account, which (within some limits) increases the total distributed income to both debt and equity holders. The tax advantage, also known as the tax shield, is only applicable if the firm is profitable. The present value of the tax shield is:

$$PV(\,tax\;shield\,) = \frac{(\,tax\;shield\,)}{r_D} = T_C \times D$$

Where T_c is the applicable tax rate and D is the debt value.

The tax shield adds to the value of the firm, so in that respect it makes sense to increase debt. But using the tax shield must not be done at the expense of the so called cost of financial distress. Indeed, high leverage ratios (D/E) for a firm may indicate that it is in trouble, thereby leading to a decrease in stock price and result in a decrease in firm value.

Financial managers should aim for an optimal leverage ratio that capitalizes on the tax shield while not indicating too much distress. Another way to look at this is to observe that r_E increases as (D/E) increases but then again, so does risk. The investor can achieve greater revenues or more losses, which is exactly what leverage achieves - it amplifies (or multiplies) gains and losses.

Going back to the WACC, the after tax WACC is[76]:

$$r_A = r_D \times (1 - T_C) \times \frac{D}{V} + r_E \times \frac{E}{V}$$

Again, the WACC calculation above assumes that the firm is wholly profitable; otherwise the tax shield cannot be used.

If the company's leverage ratio D/E changes from state 1 to state 2 (e.g., due to refinancing), then the WACC can be adjusted by calculating:

$$r_{A_1} = r_{D_1} \times \frac{D_1}{V_1} + r_{E_1} \times \frac{E_1}{V_1}$$

$$r_{E_2} = r_{A_1} + (r_{A_1} - r_{D_2}) \times \frac{D_2}{E_2}$$

$$WACC_2 = r_{A_2} = r_{D_2} \times \frac{D_2}{V_2} \times (1 - T_C) + r_{E_2} \times \frac{E_2}{V_2}$$

Where r_{A_1} is the opportunity cost of capital.

---

[76] The tax shield only applies if the firm is profitable.

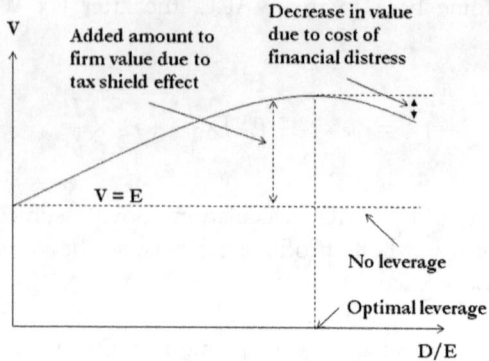

Firm market value V versus leverage ratio D/E

Valuation Methods

In this section, two firm valuation methods are discussed:

- Discounted cash flow.
- Comparable values.

Discounted Cash Flow Method

The discounted cash flow valuation method estimates the value of the firm by discounting its future cash flow (FCF) at the WACC rate. This is done by calculating[77]:

FCF = *(profit after tax but before interest)* + *depreciation*
$\qquad$ − *(capital expenditure)* − *(investment in working capital)*

---

[77] Note that capital expenditures (capex) are amounts spent on acquiring fixed assets, restoring property or adapting it to a new or different use, starting a new business, or investing in stocks or bonds.

Where investment in working capital is the change in working capital from last year, and profit after tax but before interest is:

$$EBIT \times (1 - T_C)$$

Then calculate:

$$PV = \sum_{i=1}^{n} \frac{FCF_i}{(1 + WACC)^i} + \frac{PV_n}{(1 + WACC)^n}$$

Where g is an approximation of the GDP growth rate[78] and:

$$PV_n = FCF_n + \frac{1}{WACC - g}$$

Finally, calculate:

$$E = PV - D$$

A slightly different approach to the above would be to discount the FCF to equity by r_E, which directly gives the value of E. FCF to equity is:

$$FCF_{to\ equity} = FCF - (debt\ interest) \times (1 - T_C) + (net\ debt\ issues)$$

Comparable Values Method

The comparable values method utilizes the data of

---

[78] GDP growth rate varies but may be approximated at 2-4%.

a comparable firm in order to estimate the value of the target firm.

The conditions for comparing two companies are similar risk, similar D/E ratio, and similar or same field of business. Valuation of the target firm can be done as follows:

$$(target\ V) = \frac{(comparable\ V) \times (target\ EBIT\ or\ EBITDA\ or\ Sales)}{(comparable\ EBIT\ or\ EBITDA\ or\ Sales)}$$

$$(target\ E) = (comparable\ E) = \frac{SP \times (\#\ shares) \times (target\ EPS\ or\ Sales)}{(comparable\ EPS\ or\ Sales)}$$

One can also use the WACC of a comparable firm for discounting projects of the target firm.

Capital Budgeting

Undertaking a project often requires one or more investment in equipment, recruitment, training, marketing, promotion, etc. Firms in need of new capital generally prefer to use internal funds first in order to avoid sending signals to the market about the firm's financial capabilities or general strategy.

As a second choice, firms use debt (loans, bonds). Equity is issued as a last resort[79] in the form of new shares sold to investors. This manner of proceeding is referred to as the pecking order of firm financing, which often underpins the choice of its capital budget

---

[79] Generally speaking, issuing new stock drives share price down as the market thinks managers believe the share price is overvalued.

structure or how it funds its operations.

Note that firms can also engage in financial speculation through derivatives and trading secondary stocks (the firm's and those of others).

As illustrated below, sources of funds can be broadly categorized as emanating from banks and securities markets. Those funds can also be associated with money markets, capital markets, and derivative markets. Money markets are for immediate and short term investments, while capital markets provide long term financing. We discussed derivatives earlier in this chapter.

Banks are generally proficient in analyzing credit worthiness and maintain a relatively strong oversight of their managers' performance. However, banks are usually risk averse and reluctant to lend money to risky start-up ventures.

Securities markets exhibit more flexibility, as securities can be easily traded on the markets and offer a number of alternatives to raising capital. As a result, project undertakers, such as entrepreneurs or existing firms, will usually find it easier to uncover funds for a project on the securities markets.

Obviously, investors will ask for return rates that match the risk of the project and reputation of the borrower, but it is difficult for such investors to assess the creditworthiness of parties issuing securities.

While banks typically have good systems for maintaining their own performance, securities markets discipline themselves based on the law of supply and demand.

Note that Stocks can be offered on the so called primary market upon first issuance by a firm (if the firm's stocks were not previously traded on the market, it is referred to as initial public offering - IPO), or on the secondary market, where stocks that have previously been issued are traded between investors.

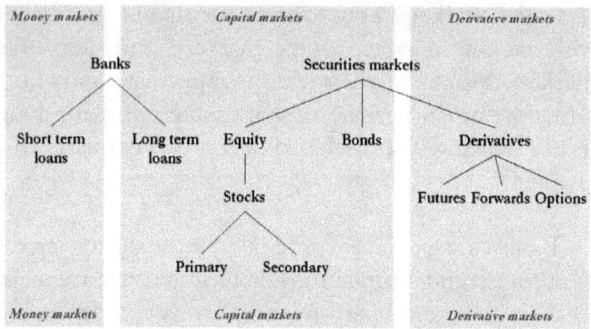

Simplified view of financial systems[80]

---

[80] Additional markets include: insurance, foreign exchange, commodities, etc.

III. ACCOUNTING

"Balanced budget requirements seem more likely to produce accounting ingenuity than genuinely balanced budgets." – Thomas Sowell

Accounting provides a common language for the analysis of financial measurements. Although the untrained individual may have difficulty grasping the vocabulary, once one masters key definitions and calculation techniques, he or she will discover solid tools which facilitate the business decision making process.

Accounting is a vast field, a profession in itself. As an MBA, perhaps the most important take away is the ability to understand financial statements, a practice known as financial accounting[81]. This chapter will cover:

---

[81] Financial accounting is typically defined as the set of activities that allow the firm to provide information about its finances. It is often distinguished from managerial or cost accounting, which is the set of methods, tools, and practices that allow managers to make decision based on the information contained in financial statements.

- Financial statements.
- Indicators of firm performance based on financial statements.

Financial Statements

Financial statements are the collection of records that illustrate the financial situation of an entity such as a business or even an individual. In their most basic form, financial statements comprise of a balance sheet, a profit and loss (P&L) statement (aka income statement), and a cash flow statement, which are examined in detail in this chapter.

It is worth noting that many organizations publish their financial statements as part of an annual report that can include several other documents including the CEO's message, analysis of the firm's financial performance, description of accounting policies[82], historical data (usually from the past five years), list of subsidiaries, information about shareholders and changes in equity, governance report and management remuneration figures, and audit reports[83].

Publicly listed companies[84] have a legal obligation to publish their financial statements on a yearly basis.

---

[82] These are the rules for reporting financial statements that the firm follows. E.g., depreciation method or methods in which earnings and expenses are recorded and reported.

[83] Audit reports list the findings of verifications of accounts that are typically performed by a neutral and reputable third party.

[84] A publicly listed company has gone through an initial public offering (IPO) and its stock is publicly available for trade on one or more stock exchange.

Privately held firms usually issue them as well, if not for public disclosure, to ensure better internal management, maintain good investor relations, and prepare tax returns and possible tax audits. Some companies also publish interim financial statements before the financial year's end. Although they are not subject to a certified audit by a neutral third party, interim financial statements can be useful in maintaining shareholder and investor confidence as well as providing information about the firm during critical times. The following subsections cover:

- Balance sheets.
- Profit and loss (P&L) statements.
- Cash flow statements.
- Consolidation of financial statements.

Balance Sheets

Balance sheets are a snapshot of a firm's assets versus its liabilities at a given point in time. Assets are valuable possessions in the form of cash; property, plant, and equipment (PP&E); monies due to be collected from third parties, etc.

Liabilities consist of debt and equity. Debt includes all future obligations resulting from past events such as loan payments, taxes, and employee benefit plans. Equity is also a liability as it reflects ownership amounts owed to investors or shareholders of the firm.

By detailing the debt and equity of the company under liabilities, balance sheets provide insight into how the firm finances its operations. The higher the debt to equity (D/E) ratio[85], the more the firm is said to be leveraged. The value of the firm is calculated as:

$$V = assets = liabilities = debt + equity$$

Assets	Liabilities
1. Current assets	1. Current debt
a. Cash	a. Accounts payable
b. Cash equivalents	b. Salaries payable
c. Inventory	c. Taxes payable
d. Accounts receivable	d. Interest payable
e. Pre-paid expenses	e. Short-term debt
2. Fixed assets	2. Long term debt
a. Property, plant, and equipment (PP&E)	a. Deferred taxes
	b. Health care costs for retired employees
b. Purchased intangibles	c. Onerous contracts
	d. Contingencies
c. Goodwill	e. Provisions
d. Investments	f. Share dividends
	3. Equity
	a. Share capital
	b. Retained earnings
	c. Convertibles

Main constituents of a balance sheet

---

[85] The mix of debt and equity is referred to as the firm's capital structure, meaning how it finances its operations. Equity comes from investors who buy stakes in the company and debt consists of loans from banks, bonds, etc. See the chapter on Corporate Finance.

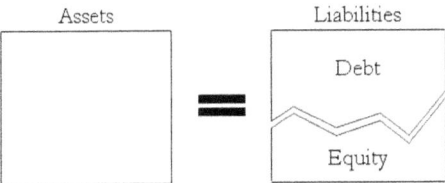

Equality between assets and liabilities

Current assets are items that are expected to be consumed in the short term such as in the upcoming year and include:

- Cash: Money that is immediately available.
- Cash equivalents: Marketable securities[86] that can be readily converted into cash.
- Inventory: Products that are in stock[87].
- Accounts receivable: Monies expected to be received from third parties.
- Pre-paid expenses: Payments already made for products, services, or assets to be obtained in the future.

Fixed assets are items that are consumed over a long period of time, e.g., equipment, furniture. They are listed at cost after deducting depreciation[88,89] and

---

[86] Tradable financial instruments such as stocks, options, derivatives, etc. See the chapter on Corporate Finance.
[87] The reasons for maintaining an inventory can include meeting anticipated demand, protecting against stock-outs, and protecting against or betting on price changes.
[88] Amortization and depreciation reflect consumption and measure wearing out. They reduce the firm's taxable revenue but are not a cash liability; they simply reflect a decrease in asset value. Depreciation of monetary assets and intangibles is referred to as amortization. Purchased or

include:

- PP&E such as land, buildings, and machinery.
- Purchased intangibles[90] which are impalpable non-monetary assets (e.g., patents, copyright, software, brands, items developed under a contract).
- Goodwill, which is the difference between the purchase value and the actual value of a purchased entity, asset, or company. For example, a firm may be worth $100 million based on its stock market price[91] but sold at $500 million because the buyer sees a large potential for future growth. Negative goodwill can occur if the purchase value ends up amounting to less than the actual asset value. Goodwill is not depreciated but is subject to a yearly impairment test[92].
- Investments that allocate monetary resources to

---

internally produced assets that are subject to depreciation are referred to as capitalized items (also see the chapter on Corporate Finance).

[89] (listed cost) = (actual cost)−(depreciation)−(accumulated impairment losses).

[90] Intangibles are not listed on the balance sheet but appear as expenses on the P&L. They do, however, become assets on the balance sheet if they are produced internally and later become a product that is commercialized and sold or purchased from another firm. In short, self-generated intangibles usually do not appear on the balance sheet whereas purchased ones do.

[91] See valuation in the chapter on Corporate Finance.

[92] Impairment is the value to be deducted due to a bad estimation of the value of purchased items or expenses (e.g., the firm purchased an asset with an estimated value of $10k, only to later find out the real value was $2k, thereby generating impairment worth $8k).

one or more projects which are expected to generate a positive return some time in the future.

Current debt encompasses items expected to be paid off with current assets in the short term, typically within the upcoming year and include:

- Accounts payable: Monies due to third parties.
- Salaries payable: Compensation due to employees.
- Taxes payable: Taxes due.
- Interest payable: Interest on loans.
- Short term debt: Debt that is due in the near future.

Long term debt is debt that is scheduled over long periods of time, and may include:

- Deferred taxes: Tax payments due over a long term schedule.
- Health care costs of retired employees: An example of future liabilities of the firm. These are amounts to be put aside for expenses the company is certain to incur as employees retire.
- Onerous contracts: Business contracts which yield a lower bottom line[93] than expected.
- Contingencies: Cash set aside for events that may or may not happen.
- Provisions: Cash set aside for events that are likely to happen without certainty as to when they will occur.
- Share dividends: Payments to be made to shareholders out of the firm's profits or reserves[94].

---

[93] Net return after cost deductions.
[94] See the chapter on Corporate Finance.

Equity refers to the shareholders' ownership of a firm's assets. It is the difference between assets and debts and therefore grows with profits and shrinks with losses incurred by the firm. Equity can take the form of:

- Share capital: Funds raised by issuing shares in return for cash or other benefits. The value reflects the amount raised, regardless of how much the stock is worth past that date (i.e., if the firm raises $1m in exchange for shares that increase in market value to $3m, the firm's share capital remains $1m).
- Retained earnings: Profit after dividend tax, share repurchase[95], or investments in future financial growth.
- Convertibles: Bonds, stocks, or other securities.

Profit and Loss (P&L) Statements

Profit and loss statements, also known as income statements, reveal the firm's net profits, a primary indicator of a company's financial performance. P&L statements reflect all transactions made in terms of revenues and expenses over a given time period, known as an accounting period (e.g., a year or a quarter) and build on this simple formula:

$$(net\ income) = revenues - expenses$$

P&L statements, therefore, can help to quickly identify shortcomings in sales performance,

---

[95] Refers to the case in which firms buy back their own shares from the market.

inadequate earning margins, or excessive costs. Some of the keywords used in these statements include:

- Cost of goods sold (COGS): Covers all costs associated with the production of goods to be sold[96].
- Material: Cost of raw or manufactured materials consumed in the production of products to be sold or services to be rendered.
- Labor: Wages paid to employees (aka payroll).
- EBIT: Earnings after expenses and before interest and taxes.
- EBITDA or gross profit: Earnings after expenses and before interest, taxes, depreciation, and amortization.
- Other operating income: Income not directly related to the company's primary field of operation.

---

[96] Limited to direct costs of production such as labor and raw materials.

		Year		
Revenues		1	2	3
	Sales[97]			
	Quarter 1			
	+ Quarter 2			
	+ Quarter 3			
	+ Quarter 4			
A	**Total sales**			
	Cost of Goods Sold			
	Material			
	+ Labor			
B	**Total COGS**			
A-B	**Gross profit (EBITDA)**			
	Other revenues[98]			
	Interest revenues			
	+ Other revenues			
C	**Total other revenues**			
A-B+C	**Total revenues**			
Expenses				
	Operating expenses			
	Rent			
	+ Utilities			
	+ Depreciation			
D	**Total operating expenses**			
Net income				
A-B+C-D	Operating profit (EBIT)			
E	Interest			
A-B+C-D-E	Net income before tax			
F	Income tax expense			
A-B+C-D-E-F	**Net income**[99]			

Sample template of a three year P&L statement

---

[97] Aka turnover.
[98] Aka non operating revenues.
[99] Aka the firm's bottom line.

Cash Flow Statements

Cash flow statements, as the name indicates, focus solely on cash transactions and detail how the firm obtains and spends its cash. These statements also range over a period of time such as a quarter or a year.

A firm generates cash from selling its assets and the goods it produces, taking loans[100], or raising equity capital. Cash expenditures go toward running the firm's operations, purchasing assets, making dividends payments, or repurchasing the firm's own stocks.

Because cash management is one of the most important elements of maintaining a firm's operations[101], managers use cash flow statements to closely monitor the company's performance. Some managers rely on daily updates, particularly when the company is experiencing difficulties, in order to ensure continued operations.

---

[100] From banks or by issuing bonds. See the chapter on Corporate Finance.
[101] Firms do not typically go out of business unless they run out of cash.

		Month	
Operating activities		**1**	**2**
	Cash received		
	Products & services		
+	Other		
A	**Total cash received**		
	Cash used		
	Labor		
+	Other		
B	**Total cash used**		
A-B	**Net operating activities**		
Investing activities			
	Cash received		
	Sale of PP&E		
+	Other		
C	**Total cash received**		
	Cash used		
	Purchase of PP&E		
+	Other		
D	**Total cash used**		
C-D	**Net investing activities**		
Financing activities			
	Cash received		
	Loans		
+	New stocks (equity)		
E	**Total cash received**		
	Cash used		
	Loan payments		
+	Stocks repurchase		
+	Dividend payments		
F	**Total cash used**		
E-F	**Net financing activities**		
	Cash at period beginning		
A-B+C-D+E-F	**Cash at period end**		

Sample template of a two months cash flow statement

Consolidation of Financial Statements

The financial statements of various inter-related firms are often consolidated so that an overall view of the entire set may be analyzed. A few consolidation methods include:

- Removing inter-company balances (e.g., sale of a parent company to a subsidiary and vice-versa and transactions between subsidiaries).
- Choosing a single representative currency.
- Aligning date ranges across the various statements.

Indicators of Firm Performance Based on Financial Statements

Financial statements can provide quick health checks on the company's performance and overall situation. Accountants employ the calculations below, also known as financial indicators. When calculating financial indicators, it is best to compare them to the values from previous accounting periods (e.g., years, quarters) as well as to those of competitors' and industry wide averages[102].

The current ratio indicates the firm's ability to pay its debts in the upcoming year. A value of 1.5 to 3 is generally considered good:

---

[102] Often categorized by industry and company size, thereby allowing for a relevant comparison to the firm under consideration.

$$(current\ ratio) = \frac{(current\ assets)}{(current\ liabilities)}$$

The quick ratio indicates the firm's ability to use its cash assets to cover its debt in the upcoming year. A value of 1 to 2 is generally considered good:

$$(quick\ ratio) = \frac{cash + (cash\ equivalents) + (accounts\ receivable)}{(current\ liabilities)}$$

The gross profit margin indicates the firm's ability to convert input (raw material, labor, etc.) into income:

$$(gross\ profit\ margin) = \frac{revenues - COGS}{revenues}$$

The debt to equity ratio (D/E) indicates the extent of the firm's leverage, meaning how much of its value is made up of debt, as opposed to equity:

$$D\!\big/\!_E = \frac{(total\ liabilities)}{(total\ equity)}$$

The debtors turnover indicates how fast the firm collects its income from customers:

$$(debtors\ turnover) = 365 \times \frac{(accounts\ receivable)}{revenues}$$

The stock turnover indicates the number of times inventory is consumed in a given year:

$$(stock\ turnover) = 2 \times \frac{COGS}{(beginning\ stock + end\ stock)}$$

The return on assets indicates the firm's performance in terms of using its assets to earn income:

$$(return\ on\ assets) = \frac{(net\ income)}{(total\ assets)}$$

The return on equity indicates the firm's ability to turn shareholder investment into profit:

$$(return\ on\ equity) = \frac{(net\ income)}{(shareholders'\ equity)}$$

The working capital[103] indicates liquidities presently available to the firm:

$$(working\ capital) = (current\ assets) - (current\ liabilities)$$

The compounded annual growth rate (CAGR) indicates the percentage in revenue growth between two moments in time i and j:

$$CAGR = (\frac{revenue_j}{revenue_i})^{\frac{1}{j-i}} - 1$$

The earnings per share (EPS) indicates the

---

[103] E.g., inventory, cash, accounts payable, accounts receivable.

payment in dividends made for each eligible stockholder:

$$EPS = \frac{(net\ income) - dividends}{(\#\ shares)}$$

The price to earnings ratio (P/E) indicates the earning potential of the stock, with a high P/E suggesting the potential for high future earnings. It is typically used to compare a firm's stock to that of other firms:

$$P\!\!\Big/\!_E = \frac{(share\ price)}{EPS}$$

IV. STRATEGY

"A satisfied customer is the best business strategy of all." –
Michael LeBoeuf

Strategic analysis identifies the choices and trade-offs that optimize long-term profitability and the approach used to create, capture, and maintain a firm's value. A successful strategy is simple, consistent, and upholds long-term objectives. Developing a strategy requires a solid understanding of the macro environment and industry in which a firm operates, investigative research on the competition, and a continual knowledge of a firm's resources, values[104], structure, competitive advantages[105], and overall mission statement[106]. This information helps managers identify the best strategy to follow including the

---

[104] A firm's values and culture are beneficial in that they set constraints and a framework for the company's business activities. They tend to increase effectiveness by setting an internal consensus.

[105] A firm enjoys a competitive advantage over others when it has an ability or resource (e.g., proprietary technology, superior knowledge, access to better raw materials) that enables it to outperform competitors and earn more in a specific market.

[106] The firm's stated objectives for what it wants to achieve and become.

strategic orientation of product and service development.

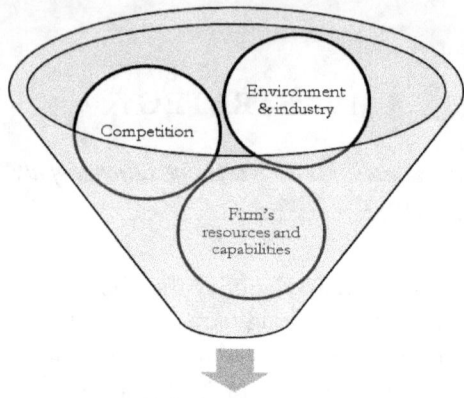

Firm strategy (product and service plans, competitive stance, etc.)

Designing firm strategy

This chapter will cover:

- Environment analysis and industry analysis.
- Competitive analysis.
- Analysis of the organization.
- Combining various strategy frameworks.
- Strategy consulting.

Environment and Industry Analysis

Several tools can guide the environment and industry analysis including:

- PESTEL framework.
- Five forces analysis.
- Opportunities and threats analysis.
- Assessment of market size and drivers.

- Cost structure analysis.

PESTEL Framework

The PESTEL[107] framework is an evaluation of high level (or macro) factors that affect the firm's business and which are beyond the firm's influence. The PESTEL's primary purpose is to rank factors in order of importance and attempt to project future changes in their level of significance. Each of the factors in a PESTEL analysis may also help in identifying opportunities for and threats to the firm. Examples of elements to consider in a PESTEL analysis cover the following[108]:

- Political:
    - Form of government, political stability, and conflicts.
    - Tax and trade policies, international relations.
- Economic:
    - GDP, investment, and consumption levels.
    - Inflation and interest rates.
    - Unemployment and wage levels.

---

[107] The PESTEL framework analyzes business conditions on the political, economic, socio-cultural, technological, environmental, and legal levels. It is also referred to as PEST (political, economic, socio-cultural, and technological analysis) or STEEP (social, technological, economic, ecological, and political/legal). Although the framework has changed over time, it is attributed to Aguilar, Francis J. in his book *Scanning the Business Environment*. New York: Macmillan Co., 1967. Print.

[108] Note that several items are also macroeconomic indicators (see the chapter on Economics).

- Socio-cultural:
  - o Fashion, lifestyles, and social fabric (ethnicities, education, age groups).
  - o Consumer buying behavior and distribution of wealth.
- Technological:
  - o Research and innovation.
  - o Standardization and legislation.
  - o Intellectual property protection issues.
- Environmental:
  - o Public sensitivity to environmental issues.
  - o Environmental protection and energy consumption laws.
- Legal:
  - o Market competition laws.
  - o Employment, health, and safety laws.

Dimension	Trend(s)	Impact
Political	Use of social networks in popular protests	Government monitoring and threats to freedom
Economic	Economic crisis	IT budget cuts, rise of online advertisement costs
Socio-cultural	Social media impact on social behavior	Invasion of privacy and digitization of human relations
Technological	Cloud computing, cyber warfare	Specialization and outsourcing to expert firms
Environmental	Go green	Budget allocations
Legal	Security and privacy	New laws and cost of compliance

Example PESTEL analysis for the Internet field

Using the macro environmental analysis, managers can classify the factors in terms of their importance to the firm as well predict changes in their relevance over time.

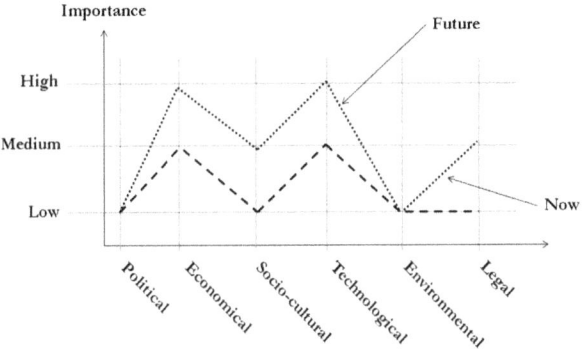

Sample assessment of PESTEL factors for a firm

Five Forces Analysis

An industry analysis aims to understand the dynamics of a given industry in order to determine the challenges associated with entering the field, the intensity of competition, success elements, and expected profits. The five forces analysis, initially explained by Michael Porter[109], is a popular method of analyzing industries and attempts to answer the following questions:

- What profits can be expected upon entering this industry?
- What are the power balances in this industry and

[109] Porter, Michael E. "How Competitive Forces Shape Strategy." Harvard Business Review 57, March–April 1979: 86-93.

which competitors may threaten profits?
- What are the barriers of entry for this industry?

The five forces analysis examines the bargaining power of buyers and suppliers, the threat posed by substitute offerings from competitors and new entrants, and the intensity of competition in the industry.

Bargaining Power of Buyers

Buyers are the consumers (individuals, firms, governments, and other organizations) of an industry's product and service offerings. Some factors that can influence buyers' bargaining power include:

- Weight of a buyer in terms of overall contribution to a firm's sales volume. A buyer who contributes to a substantial part of a firm's revenue will naturally be in a strong negotiation position.
- Availability of substitutes and distinctive features of offerings. Buyers can easily switch from one commodity[110] provider to another, but may be less inclined to do so, and indeed at times stuck with one provider, in cases of special proprietary technologies or other unique aspects of the offering.
- Switching costs, which are incurred when changing providers[111].

---

[110] A commodity is a good that cannot be easily differentiated (e.g., water).
[111] The cost in money, time, or resources as well as the potential risks of switching from one good to another.

Bargaining Power of Suppliers

Suppliers are those entities that provide inputs[112] into the production process of industry competitors. Determinants of supplier power include:

- The competitive rivalry in the supplier's industry. The more competitive the industry, the less power the supplier has to negotiate profit margins for their offering. Conversely, if the industry is concentrated in the hands of a few large players, the supplier has a better ability to negotiate higher profit margins.
- The switching costs of changing suppliers.
- The supplier's level of dependence on the firm it supplies its goods to. The higher (lower) the proportion of a supplier's sale to a firm, the less (more) bargaining power that supplier will have[113].

Threat of New Entrants

As the name indicates, new entrants are firms that decide to enter the industry under consideration by launching competitive offerings. This causes increased industry fragmentation because more choices will be available to consumers. The result is reduced profitability for all firms competing in that particular market.

Barriers to entry are the obstacles standing in the

---

[112] E.g., raw materials, labor, services, or distribution channels.

[113] Suppliers and their clients can sometimes enter into a so called mutual hostage situation in which both parties depend on the other.

way of firms who wish to enter the industry. The lower the barriers, the easier it is to enter and vice-versa. Barriers to entry into an industry include:

- Economies of scale which give production cost advantages to incumbents[114].
- Capital requirements for entry.
- Access to raw materials.
- Consumer switching costs associated with adopting a new product or service.
- Brand name of incumbents and difficulty marketing a new offering.
- Existing market presence of incumbents.
- Knowhow and proprietary technologies.
- Business alliances (suppliers, distributors, etc.).
- Possible retaliation from incumbents[115].
- Government regulations and subsidies.

Threat of Substitutes

Substitutes of a firm's offering are similar goods sold by incumbents in the industry that can take away from sales volume and market share as well as drive profit margins down as a result of price reductions. Factors which impact the threat of substitutes are:

- Switching costs.
- Consumer tendency to switch.
- Additional features and price points.

---

[114] Firms already operating in the industry.
[115] E.g., when Google entered the desktop application field (albeit in cloud based format), Microsoft allocated resources to its search engine Bing, a move that many qualified as retaliatory.

Intensity of Competition

The intensity of competition is influenced by:

- Market size and growth patterns; the larger the market, the more potential space for competitors.
- Consumer loyalty and switching frequency.
- Prices and profit margins.
- Industry fragmentation[116].
- Exit barriers[117].

Opportunities and Threats

Opportunities and threats are part of what is commonly referred to as the SWOT analysis (strengths, weaknesses, opportunities, and threats). While opportunities and threats stem from the business environment and industry under consideration, strengths and weaknesses relate to the study of the organization itself.

An opportunities analysis identifies potential gaps in the market that the firm can exploit, possibilities of acquiring or merging with other companies, and market entry opportunities. It can also be used to assess potential market size and growth prospects as well as identify customer adoption drivers or obstacles. A threats analysis attempts to single out competitor strategies that may affect the firm's

---

[116] The more competitors, the more intense the competition.
[117] The cost of stopping production. E.g., penalties for contract termination, negative impact on brand image, and difficulty in recovering capital investments.

business (e.g., mergers, acquisitions, or market expansions). It can include the threat of unfavorable legislation or that of increased operating costs due to dependence on unreliable suppliers. In short, both the opportunities and threats analysis will consider factors that may impact the firm at the macroeconomic context as well as the industry in which the firm operates.

Assessment of Market Size and Drivers

A market size estimation follows the demand forecasting techniques described in the chapter on Marketing. Market drivers are the decision factors that impact customer purchase choices in the industry under consideration and can include both positive and negative motivational elements. For example, a coffee shop owner may be positively driven to offer free wireless Internet access to patrons but may fear incurring excessive costs. An Internet service provider that understands these drivers and obstacles will craft a value proposition that enables easy to use and high quality Internet access to patrons while providing tools and reports to allow shop owners to monitor and control costs (e.g., excessive bandwidth usage).

Cost Structure Analysis

A cost structure analysis aims to examine the cost components that underpin a firm's operations. By breaking down costs into their constituents and classifying them into fixed and variable costs, managers can identify improvement opportunities and areas with a higher margin potential.

5%	Utilities
25%	Rent
10%	Technology
20%	Administration
35%	Labor

| X-ray film | 3% |
| Medical supplies | 2% |

Fixed costs   **Variable costs**

Example cost structure analysis of a medical radiology unit

A popular method of examining a firm's cost structure is the value chain analysis, which was also first described by Michael Porter[118]. This framework structures the cost analysis along a firm's typical functions and activities such as human resource management, technology, operations, and marketing. As such, Porter's tool helps determine how a firm and the industry within which it operates are organized in terms of cost components, margins, and differentiation potential. Specifically, the value chain analysis deconstructs the costs of doing business in a certain industry by:

---

[118] Porter, Michael E. *Competitive Advantage: Creating and Sustaining Superior Performance.* New York, N.Y.: Free Press Collier Macmillan, 1985. Print.

- Identifying cost components.
- Benchmarking the firm's operations versus competitors'.
- Identifying cost drivers.
- Identifying opportunities to reduce costs.
- Identifying differentiation potential by uncovering unique aspects of each activity.

The value chain analysis is useful in analyzing the industry as a whole and the firm itself (as part of the analysis of the organization). It can also be used to examine the interactions of firms which engage in trade or form partnerships in order to deliver a finished good to customers.

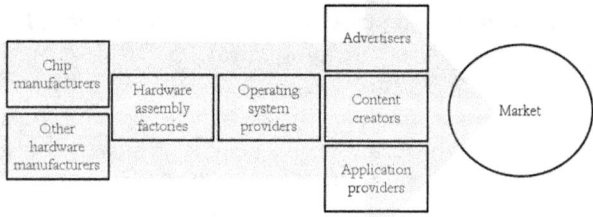

Value chain in the tablet computing industry

Managers can also perform an industry profit pool analysis to determine profit margins for various activities or offerings within the scope of a particular industry. This can help direct the firm's focus as managers allocate the firm's resources to the highest profit making sectors.

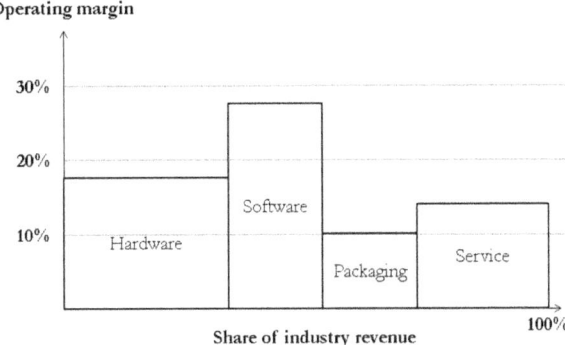

Example of industry profit pool analysis

Competitive Analysis

The competitive analysis presents a picture of competitors' current and planned activities, the market segments they target, and their methods of conducting business. With this knowledge, the firm can adjust its strategy to exploit market gaps and compete. The frameworks described in previous sections (PESTEL, five forces, and opportunities and threats) can all feed data into the competitive analysis, which may involve:

- Intelligence gathering from:
  - Patent applications.
  - Published reports.
  - Business databases.
  - Inferral of information (e.g., factory tours[119]).
- Competitive strategy analysis:

---

[119] Things to look at include location of the factory, supplier trucks, inventory size, notice boards, workstations, recent changes, etc.

- o Understanding competitors' business models.
  - o Following marketing campaigns.
  - o Staying updated on news about alliances, acquisitions, etc.
- The organizations themselves:
  - o Their history.
  - o Their stated mission and values.
- Cost structure analysis:
  - o Understanding how competitors' value chains are organized.
  - o Comparing with competitors' cost structures.
  - o Determining competitors' strengths.

Using this information, managers can group similar market offerings to identify market gaps, market entry barriers, and sustainability of a business. This can be achieved by comparing the firm's product with those of competitors on a two dimensional grid featuring relevant metrics, resulting in a cluster analysis[120].

When a firm fills a market gap that is not addressed by competitors, it is said to gain first mover advantage (FMA) which can translate into competitive advantage if the firm manages to use its move to erect barriers to entry[121]. Firms that later mimic a first mover sometimes benefit from so called second mover advantage, particularly if the first mover has not been able to capitalize on the early move to protect its share of the market. This can occur if the

---

[120] Aka perceptual mapping or strategic grouping analysis.
[121] E.g., build market share, brand recognition, knowhow, etc.

first mover had to spend a large portion of its capital to enter the new market, so much so that profits were not sufficient to make the business case viable. The second mover will then be able to capture the value previously created[122] to turn the situation into a profitable opportunity.

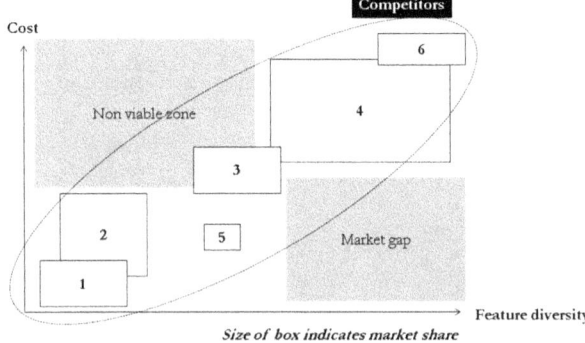

Example of a cluster analysis

Analysis of the Organization

An analysis of the organization aims at determining functional strategies for the firm, meaning how it will go about running its business and allocating its focus in light of market conditions and competitors' behavior. Functional strategies can therefore cover (amongst others):

- Corporate strategy: Defines the sector in which the firm will compete.
- Business strategy: Addresses how to compete.

---

[122] E.g., discounted purchase of investment, copying knowhow.

- Financial strategy: Determines how the firm will fund its operations (equity, debt, etc.).
- Organizational strategy: Tackles the culture, recruitment approach, compensation methods, and related topics[123].
- Production strategy: Establishes what to make and what materials are needed in the production of goods[124].

The following section focuses on corporate and business strategies.

Corporate Strategy

Choosing an industry to compete in will essentially build on the macro level, industry, and competitor analyses, but it must also relate external opportunities to the firm's core competences, which will help identify activities that give the firm a competitive advantage. Core competences are identified by examining:

- Strengths and weaknesses of the firm (which add to opportunities and threats identified in the macro level and industry analysis and therefore complete the SWOT analysis).
- Firm resources[125] including:
  - o Tangibles: Cash, borrowing power, real estate, equipment.
  - o Human assets: Know-how, motivation, loyalty.

---

[123] See the chapter on Organizational Behavior.
[124] See the chapter on Operations Management.
[125] Aka resource based view (RBV) of the firm.

- o Intangibles: Patents, copyrights, brands, culture.
- VRIO assets that are:
  - o **V**aluable, meaning they can generate profit for the firm if put to good use.
  - o **R**are, meaning not easily accessible to competitors.
  - o Difficult (or costly) to **I**mitate.
  - o Exploited or capable of being exploited by the **O**rganization.

A VRIO asset analysis can help managers identify firm competencies or resources that can underpin a sustained long term competitive advantage. For example, a patent that protects the intellectual property of a valuable invention and that the firm can exploit will constitute a VRIO asset, as it satisfies all four conditions and can result in a long term competitive advantage (at least for the duration of the patent's life[126]). The VRIO assets fit within the strengths analysis of the firm.

Business Strategy

Business strategy[127] defines how the firm will compete and sustain a competitive advantage. Some of the tools and frameworks used to develop business strategy include:

- Cost structure analysis (described above).

---

[126] Varies depending on the category of the invention and the jurisdiction, but is generally 20 years from the date of initial filing.
[127] Aka competitive strategy.

- Generic strategies.
- Blue Ocean Strategies®.

Generic Strategies

Elaborated by Michael Porter[128], generic strategies can either focus on cost leadership or differentiation[129]. In the first case, the firm competes on price, whereas in the second, it competes on the specificity of the offering and avoids direct price competition.

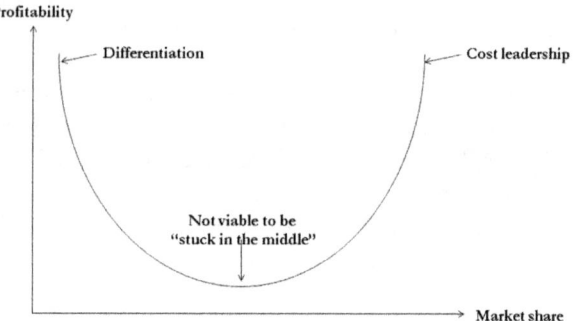

Profitability versus market share for generic strategies

As illustrated above, firms that attempt to compete on price as well as differentiation often underperform

---

[128] Porter, Michael E. *Competitive Strategy: Techniques for Analyzing Industries and Competitors.* New York, N.Y.: Free Press, 1980. Print.
[129] Most analyses of generic strategies also mention focus strategy as an alternative. This simply refers to the case in which a firm concentrates on a niche market in the particular industry; however, the trade-off between cost and differentiation will typically still hold.

compared with those that try to achieve one of the two. The firm's cost structure analysis can be useful in carrying out its cost leadership strategy because it can help lower production costs. In addition, the experience curve[130] contributes to cost factors as costs of production decrease with time and volume, which allows the firm to lower its offering's selling price accordingly.

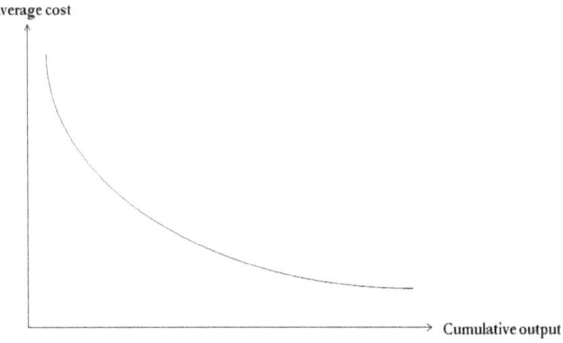

Illustration of the experience curve

Blue Ocean Strategy®

Coined by W. Kim Chan and Renée Mauborgne[131], Blue Ocean Strategy® is an approach in which a firm targets untapped market gaps rather than competing head to head with other firms in exploited sectors.

---

[130] Increasingly relevant as the firm's market share, experience, and output levels increase.
[131] Kim, W C., and Mauborgne, Renée. *Blue Ocean Strategy: How to Create Uncontested Market Space and Make the Competition Irrelevant.* Boston, Mass: Harvard Business School Press, 2005. Print.

Firms that create and capture the value of a Blue Ocean Strategy® gain a competitive advantage because they create new market demand (i.e., a blue or empty ocean).

Firms can achieve this by thinking of the business as extending beyond its traditional niche of competitors, customers, or target areas, and then putting together an unprecedented value proposition that builds on the firm's capabilities in its traditional field of business to allow it to compete in another space. For example, when Apple launched the iPod, it was no longer targeting the computing industry (its traditional focus), but had entered the entertainment sector, albeit with an unprecedented offering. The iPod put Apple in competition with music and movie sellers; however, it had a unique offering (the combination of the iPod and iTunes store) which no other competitor boasted.

Tools used to devise a Blue Ocean Strategy® include:

- The strategy value canvas, which positions firms against each other in terms of competitive factors such as feature set, price, service level, etc.
- The ERRC framework (eliminate, raise, reduce, or create differentiators.). Starting with a strategic value canvas, managers can craft a distinctive value proposition that adopts a unique combination of the dimensions of the canvas.

Practically speaking, Blue Ocean Strategy® allows firms to adopt both cost leadership and differentiation strategies as there is virtually no competition. Obviously, if a firm creates a new market but fails to erect solid barriers to entry, other players will eventually follow suit, thus turning the "blue ocean" into a "red ocean" and generic strategies will again apply.

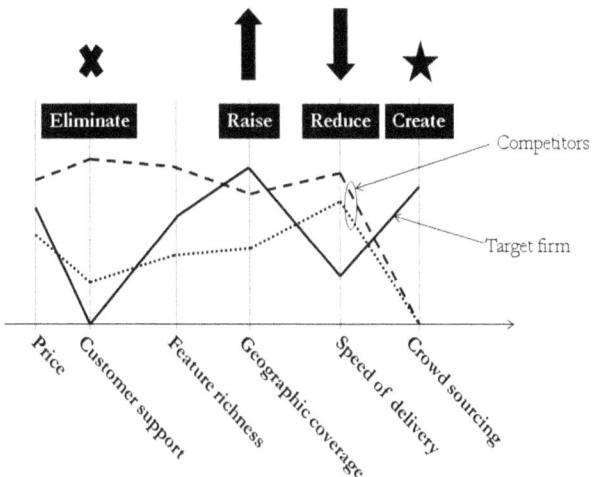

The ERRC framework on a strategy canvas

Once a Blue Ocean Strategy® is identified and implemented, it is essential that a firm erect barriers to entry in order to maintain its advantage and prevent other firms from entering the field and/or adopting a similar business model or production process.

Combining Various Strategy Frameworks

After completing the various analyses described above, it is always beneficial for managers to investigate alternative scenarios which consider possible changes in future expectations in terms of profits, competitor behavior, industry variations, and technological advancements. The first phase is to devise alternative scenarios by:

- Identifying parameters that are subject to change.
- Estimating the various cases or possibilities for each of those parameters.
- Thinking of the system as a whole which can help remove impossible or unlikely combinations of outcomes.
- Zooming in on a few possible scenarios.

Once alternative scenarios have been identified, managers can[132]:

- Obtain expert opinions on change possibilities, and aim for rough estimations for various quantifiable events or a range of possibilities for unquantifiable ones.
- With quantifiable parameters, perform sensitivity analyses which assign known or estimated probability patterns to parameters that may change, and run simulations in order to zoom in on a range or array of outcome values (e.g., profit and loss analysis).
- With unquantifiable parameters, attempt to use the scenarios and options identified to determine the potential impact on the firm and how to avoid threats while embracing opportunities.

Strategy Consulting

Management consulting firms can broadly be classified into two types: business process and technology consulting and strategy consulting.

The first implements solutions that have already

---

[132] See the chapter on Quantitative Analysis.

been put in place for previous clients. The firm's goal is to help customers implement the target solution by making recommendations based on the consultants' direct knowledge of the field.

Strategy consulting firms, on the other hand, devise new ways to solve problems by building on their experience from other industries or fields of practice. Strategy firms usually have shorter mandates than business process and technology firms and therefore work quickly to deliver results by developing hypotheses and testing and adjusting them through multiple iterations[133].

The best way to understand the work done by consulting firms, particularly those that focus on strategy mandates, is to look at various case studies. A case study presents a problem similar to one which a consultancy handles. After analyzing the available information, the reader is asked to propose a solution. Topics include:

- Profit improvement.
- Industry analysis.
- Market entry.

When working on such cases (for example, during an interview), it is best to:

- Examine and compare past trends.
- Plot data on graphs to better understand the problem.
- Segment and categorize data instead of using

---

[133] This is referred to as the positivist approach.

averages (e.g., by revenue, demographics, region, etc.).

- Formulate practical and actionable recommendations while being diplomatic with the client.
- Briefly describe next steps.
- Share estimates of KPIs[134] associated with the recommendations (e.g., cut costs by 18%).
- Identify the risks of following the recommended plan.

Profit Improvement

As the name implies, profit improvement cases aim to help a client boost profits. A good approach to tackling such cases is to structure the solution based on the equation:

$$profits = revenues - costs$$
$$= [price - (variable\ costs)] \times quantity - (fixed\ costs)$$

As a result, one will have to consider ways to increase revenues, decrease costs, or both.

Increasing revenues can be achieved by:

- Looking at factors that impact price:
  - Can the price be changed through differentiation?
  - What is the pricing strategy (e.g., cost plus, market based, is it a commodity product)?

---

[134] Key performance indicators. See the chapter on Quantitative Analysis.

- Looking at factors that impact sales volume:
    - Market size, growth perspectives, competitive landscape, and market shares to determine if sales growth is possible.
- Purchase drivers:
    - How to sell more to existing customers?
    - How to acquire new customers?

Thinking frameworks to decrease costs include:

- Cost structure analysis and an examination of primary cost contributors.
- Benchmarking versus competitors.

Industry Analysis

This type of case aims at determining the structure or attractiveness of an industry. Typical elements to look at when solving such a case include:

- The market:
    - Examine market size, growth, and margins by segment, with a focus on key segments.
    - Look at any macro level factors that could have an impact (e.g., PESTEL analysis).
    - Identify which organization has the power (e.g., five forces analysis).
    - Evaluate threats and opportunities.
    - Identify barriers to entry.
    - Analyze cost structure and industry profit pool distribution.
- The competition:
    - Look at top competitors and market shares.
    - Determine whether the competition is fragmented, therefore allowing for easier market entry, or dominated by a few players with high barriers to market entry.

o   Assess potential reaction to entry.

Market Entry

This type of case is similar to an industry analysis case and focuses on determining if conditions are suitable for market entry. In addition to examining the same aspects of an industry analysis case, one can also assess the following:

- The marketing mix (product, place, price, promotion).
- The customers:
  - o Segments (size, profitability, growth projections, needs, price sensitivity, disposable income).
  - o Drivers of purchase (price, product, place, promotion) per segment.
- The product:
  - o Features and benefits.
  - o Differentiation possibilities.
  - o Possibility of co-creating markets by selling complementary products.
- Methods of market entry:
  - o Build, acquire, or enter into a joint venture.
  - o Adopt a sprinkler approach (launching in multiple markets simultaneously) or a water fall approach (a sequential launch in various markets).
  - o License out or sell patents (if the market is not attractive and/or out of the firm's scope).
- Cost/benefit:
  - o Breakeven point.
  - o Best/worst cases.
  - o Payback period.
  - o Capabilities and synergy with the firm.

V. MARKETING

"Progress lies not in enhancing what is, but in advancing toward what will be." – Khalil Gibran

The goal of marketing is to create demand for a certain offering. Marketers[135] identify customer needs, craft a corresponding product or service, and then determine how to communicate that value proposition to target consumers. Marketing communication covers: choice of communication medium (e.g., TV, newspaper, Internet campaigns), timing, and the message itself, particularly in terms of finding the appropriate strategies to capture the buyers' attention, stimulate their interest, build their desire to purchase, and finally, ensure they take action by placing an order[136]. This chapter will cover:

- Marketing management.
- Customer relationship management.
- Product and service line management.

---

[135] Individuals who perform the set of tasks associated with the marketing function.

[136] A framework known as AIDA, which stands for attention, interest, desire, and action. A similar framework is UACCA, which stands for, unawareness, awareness, comprehension, conviction, and action.

- Brand management.

Marketing Management

Marketing management pertains to the activities involved with organizing a firm's marketing activities. The following topics are discussed in this section:

- Approach to marketing.
- Marketing budgets.

Approach to Marketing

A firm's marketing activities must be performed with a strong attention to target customers, competitors, and the overall environment within which the company operates. This approach, referred to as market orientation, has been proven to increase a firm's profits, particularly by placing consumer needs at the forefront of business thinking[137]. Obviously, maintaining a focus on external factors must not come at the expense of the firm's own long term strategies and objectives. Managers therefore need to maintain both an outward and inward view.

The market orientation approach incorporates information gathering and transparency. Marketers collect information by talking to customers, conducting ethnography studies[138] to observe

---

[137] Narver, J.C. & Slater, S.F. (1990). The effect of a market orientation on business profitability. Journal of Marketing, 54(4): 20-34.

[138] Ethnography is the qualitative analysis of consumer behavior which aims to identify practical uses of products,

customers and how they use a given product (or those of competitors), listening to the firm's employees (e.g., researchers, developers, and account managers), and performing market analyses (e.g., competitors behavior, market size, and growth). The collected information is then disseminated throughout the firm using presentations, reports, and/or job rotations so that consumer needs and market gaps are accurately identified. Various firm stakeholders are brought up to speed on the latest advancements within the company (e.g., research and development, operations processes).

Through employee and stakeholder awareness, the flow of information described above can help pave the way for the extension of existing product or service offerings or the identification of new ones. The novel or modified offerings may echo existing consumer needs as well as create a new demand[139].

Lastly, the marketing approach must be applied across the firm and to all its activities. Managerial commitment must be secured and relevant communication channels and overall synergies must be setup within the company before the successful creation and launch of a product or service.

---

user preferences, etc. Today, digital ethnography is performed using electronic means such as server side behavioral tracking of various Internet content and service providers.

[139] E.g., Apple's iPod, iPhone, and iPad created a demand among a consumer base which had not perceived a need for such electronic items before their launch.

Marketing Budgets

The length of time for a new product to be adopted may vary in different market segments defined by countries, age groups, demographics, etc. While some products become rapidly popular, others may take years or even decades to be adopted[140]. As a result, marketing efforts must be focused, sustained, and consistent.

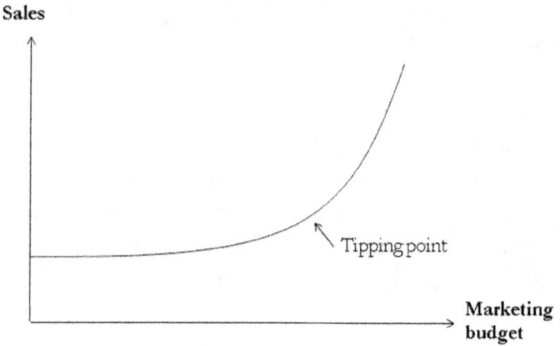

Adoption and cross of the chasm for new products

Firms usually benefit from adhering to strict budget allocations for marketing activities regardless of the performance of the product (at least until the opportunity for the offering to gain market adoption has passed). Consequently, allocating marketing budgets as a percentage of product sales is

---

[140] See for example http://www.karlhartig.com/chart/techhouse.pdf for an illustration of household penetration for some consumer-electronics products in the U.S. from 1920–1998.

inappropriate; only through persistent long term investment will marketing pay off and product sales escalate.

Customer Relationship Management

Customer relationship management (CRM) is the set of tools and practices that enable mutually beneficial interaction between a firm and its customer base. Good CRM entails establishing proper communication channels with customers and striving for customer satisfaction. The latter is achieved by performing at levels exceeding customer expectations[141]:

satisfaction = performance - expectations

Customer satisfaction is believed to increase loyalty[142], grow the existing customer base, and decrease acquisition costs[143]. The net result is augmented profits. Common practices utilized in an

---

[141] A practical tip for dealing with a customer is under-promising and over-delivering.

[142] A 5% increase in loyalty has been shown to escalate profits by 25-85%. Note, however, that the relationship between loyalty and profits is not a linear one. In fact, research has shown that there are optimum levels of customer loyalty to aim for (through resource allocation in terms of time and money) (Reichheld, Frederick F., and Sasser Jr., W. Earl. "Zero Defections: Quality Comes to Services." Harvard Business Review September–October (1990): 3-6).

[143] Because customers will develop a trust relationship with the brand and buy other items without comparing them to similar offerings in the market.

effort to manage and exceed customer expectations include:

- Empowering employees[144].
- Reducing centralization and allowing employees to generate customer satisfaction on the spot.
- Treating customers with respect and showing them empathy.
- Taking into account the customer's voice when making decisions.
- Maintaining transparency and reliability in dealing with complaints and issues[145].
- Maintaining multiple customer contact points.
- Providing varied, numerous and easily accessible channels for customer complaints.

Some of the metrics relating to CRM assess the customer and relationship capitals of the firm based on:

- Customer retention rates through repeat sales.
- Existing customer referrals which generate new ones.
- Propensity of customers to switch to competitors (e.g., due to deals and rebates).

---

[144] Managers must remember that cost of acquisition is high, meaning that when a potential new customer walks into the store or solicits information about a product, the firm needs to ensure the employees dealing with the customer have received the proper training and have adequate tools at their disposal with which to obtain the customer's business.

[145] E.g., avoid broken promises, show concern, and quickly respond.

- Willingness of customers to pay more for the same product or service.
- Conduct of customers when problems arise (e.g., complain to provider, commence litigation, or switch to competition).

In fact, one simple key performance indicator (KPI) of the firm's performance in managing its relations with customers is the Net Promotion Score (NPS). The NPS is calculated by constantly sampling customers with a "yes-no" question about whether they would refer the product or service to a friend. If each "yes" answer is mapped to a value of 1 and "no" answers are mapped to a value of 0, the sum of such values divided by the total number of people sampled will yield the NPS.

Firms must try to detect and avoid the so called "leaky bucket situation" in which efforts are applied to gain more customers, while existing customers are neglected to the point that they defect. Given the high cost of customer acquisition[146] and the low cost to resell, up sell, or cross sell[147] to existing customers, it only makes sense to direct a good portion of CRM efforts into retaining existing customers in order to

---

[146] E.g., advertising, promotions.

[147] Up selling markets complementary or add-on products to a previous purchase, while cross selling engages the same customer to purchase a different product. The cost of selling to an existing customer is typically lower than selling to new customers because new customers need to be convinced to make a purchase, whereas existing customers are familiar with the company and generally require less convincing to buy a product or service.

sustain and increase profits. The point is to strike a balance between acquiring new customers and keeping existing ones, given the estimated cost and return in each case.

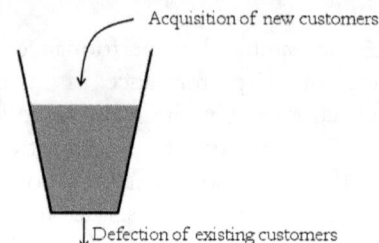

Leaky bucket principle applied to CRM

Managers may analyze the current and potential customer base more thoroughly in order to determine how to allocate budgets using factors such as:

- Customer Lifetime Value (CLV)[148].
- Risk of defection, estimated by looking at complaints, return rate, events that may have caused dissatisfaction, etc.
- Cost to retain and acquire customers[149].
- Portion of the budget earmarked for retention and/or acquisition.

Given the relationship between the cost of retaining existing customers and expected profits and the relationship between the cost of acquiring new

---

[148] Customer Lifetime Value or Lifetime Customer Value (LCV) is the net present value of all future estimated purchases by a given customer.
[149] E.g., marketing campaigns, follow up calls, promotions, brand maintenance, etc.

customers and expected profits, the goal is to find the optimal proportion of resource allocation between the cost to retain and the cost to acquire so that profits are maximized and budget constraints are met.

Product and Service Line Management

Product management is a function that sits at the intersection of strategy and marketing. Product managers interface with external and internal stakeholders in an effort to determine compelling value propositions, corresponding target markets, and commercialization plans.

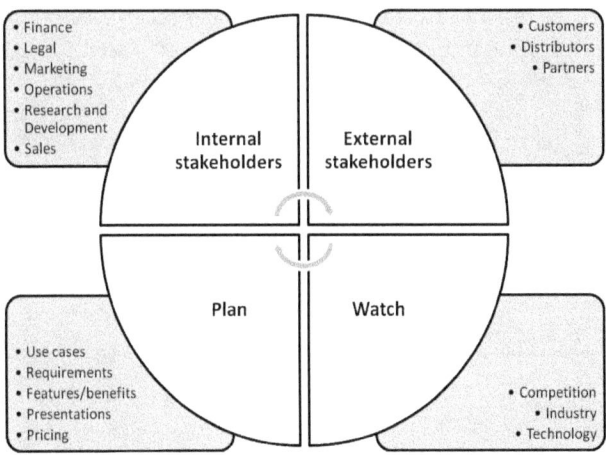

The Product Management functions

Product managers accompany the product or service throughout its lifecycle, from initial development to decline and retirement, including:

- Introduction: The initial launch of the product (or service); adoption time varies depending on market dynamics[150].

- Growth: In this phase, sales increase and multiple firms may develop an interest to enter the market. The result may be a proliferation of offerings from several vendors with a competitive focus on differentiation[151]. Products may be similar in function but diverse in terms of features, appearance, and compatibility.

- Maturity: When the industry's structure somewhat settles down among known producers and standard offerings, firms initiate a price competition. This is a result of sales volumes accelerating the incline along the experience curve[152], thereby reducing production costs.

- Decline: With evolving technology, consumer tastes, and overall changes in the industry, sales will decline until the product or service is retired.

---

[150] Marketers sometimes refer to historical adoption rates (diffusion rates) for different customer segments or geographic areas in order to decide launch strategies. This is because some people may be more inclined to adopt certain types of products than others (e.g., technologists may buy new computing devices earlier than the mass public).

[151] See the chapter on Strategy.

[152] This becomes more relevant as the firm's market share, experience, and output levels increase. This is discussed in more detail in the chapter on Strategy.

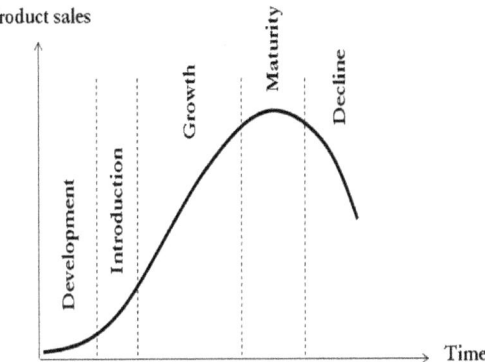

Illustration of a typical product lifecycle (PLC)

In the following subsections, the methods that product managers apply in the different PLC stages are discussed in terms of:

- Value creation.
- Value capture.

Value Creation

Technologies, practices, and markets are constantly emerging and evolving, thereby presenting firms with continual opportunities for improvement and/or innovation. Managers much keep a close eye on these progressions in order to lead with them or at least embrace them in due time.

A market-driven product development approach implies incremental changes based on customer feedback. However, firms must not let every new product idea originate from their customers; therefore, it is essential to also maintain the market-driving approach as a key strategic component of product planning. This type of approach stems from radical changes based on technological innovations and is instrumental in convincing consumers to purchase new products that they did not think or know they needed.

Value Creation Practices

Value creation practices primarily revolve around people management and the exchange of information. In terms of people management, hard rules, lack of direction, and pessimism kill creativity. On the other hand, managing workloads so employees can step back (even to the point of boredom) and see the big picture can be an effective trigger for creativity. Deadlines can also serve to be beneficial, although care must be taken in terms of timing and ability of resources to deliver, as simulated deadlines[153] become counterproductive.

To enable the prolific exchange of information, managers should aim to connect resources, rotate job assignments, encourage cross departmental collaboration in order to link various groups within the company, and leverage multi-talented employees who can bridge across disciplines (this is something MBAs usually excel at). Creating structured conflict[154] can sometimes build creative momentum by forcing individuals and groups to further refine their ideas and substantiate their arguments. In addition, the use of

---

[153] An imposed and unjustified time limit for finishing a task.

[154] A constructive discussion of ideas rather than personal clashes. See the chapter on Organizational Behavior.

Information Technology[155] for data dissemination can encourage groups within the firm to contribute or become inspired to improve their own work. Such practices can result in the following models of innovation:

- Incremental innovation: Improving existing products or services.
- Next generation innovation: Improving existing products or services utilizing significant evolutionary processes.
- Radical innovation: Totally new and never used before.

To measure creativity levels in a firm, managers rely on metrics for innovation performance including:

- Percentage of sales versus the time when underlying ideas were coined; the age distribution of currently commercialized products can indicate the creative level of a firm.
- Average time to market an innovation.
- Percentage of the budget allocated to research and development.
- Number of patent applications per year.

Innovation is typically stronger in a firm that employs the best practices and tools with which to foster value creation; yet innovations only yield a return if managers know how to create and capture value from them. Managers must keep in mind that innovation is not an objective by itself and that it is

---

[155] E.g., Wikis, blogs, shared databases.

only relevant if it eventually contributes to the firm's profits. As a result, managers must attempt to link innovation metrics to overall corporate performance, as measured in financial terms.

Value Creation Tools and Frameworks

There are many tools and frameworks that assist in identifying novel ways of delivering a service or building a new product. It is best to use a combination of tools, perhaps by feeding the results of one into the other.

Strategy analysis tools can be utilized to identify market gaps or different value propositions compared to the competition. In fact, determining the offering begins with market research, followed by defining a value proposition. The process is not necessarily linear as managers often adjust the offering based on new data, customer surveys, and/or pilot projects. The goal of market research is to understand the overall dynamics of a firm's operations, recognize customer needs, analyze the competition, and identify opportunities.

To devise a product strategy, product managers should collect data from throughout the firm as well as from customers and the market. Internal data collection must rely on strong communication channels and frequent interactions, and methods must be setup in which customers can easily provide feedback such as face to face meetings or incentives to share opinions (e.g., rebate incentives or early use of prototypes). Finally, product managers must frequently employ market studies which collect data from publicly available sources or specialized market research firms. With this information, marketers can attempt to create a general understanding of the target market before narrowing in on specifics such as market growth perspectives and customer segmentation. Areas in which to gather information include:

- General market conditions:
    - Macro level view[156].
    - High level growth perspectives (e.g., using economic indicators[157]).
    - Threats and opportunities.
- Market dynamics:
    - Trends such as interests and concerns of stakeholders in the industry, and consolidations through mergers and acquisitions.
    - Factors that affect consumer decision making.
    - Challenges facing entities that operate in the target market.
- Gap analysis:
    - Competitors (offerings, market share, strengths and weaknesses).
    - Unfulfilled needs in the market (what do customers long for but cannot get from competitors and what are the success factors for adoption of offerings).

There are two ways to gather data for market research: either use existing data (secondary market information) or conduct the research directly (and

---

[156] E.g., PESTEL analysis.
[157] E.g., Gross Domestic Product (GPD), Consumer Confidence Index (CCI), Consumer Price Index (CPI), etc.

build so called primary market information). A market research initiative will benefit from the following approach:

- Define the objectives and deliverables.
- Limit the scope.
- Decide how information will be collected.
- Allocate a budget for the effort.
- Gather data.
- Perform the analysis.

When gathering secondary market information, a marketer can use sources such as:

- Internet search engines.
- Public libraries.
- Specialized databases (e.g., www.sec.gov[158], www.uspto.gov[159], and www.oecd.org).
- Reports from market research firms and market report providers[160] (e.g., www.gatner.com, www.marketresearch.com, and www.forrester.com).
- Government and non-government organization (NGO) portals that provide economic and market indicators.

Some web resources track keyword searches and popular web page lookups. Marketers working on

---

[158] Provides financial information on publicly listed companies.
[159] Provides intellectual property information which may give insight into competitors' product or service strategies.
[160] Insight and sample data are often provided free of charge.

confidential initiatives must exercise care when using third party databases, particularly those of competitors'.

Collecting primary market information may involve the following:

- Performing online surveys[161] (e.g., using web tools such as www.surveymonkey.com, or docs.google.com).
- Conducting in person surveys (e.g., at malls, in focus groups).
- Conducting telephone interviews (e.g., with existing customer contacts).

Brainstorming can also be a powerful tool, as it allows participants to identify new concepts or thoughts. The successes of brainstorming sessions depend on how well they are managed; the following guidelines may help in that respect:

- Set and announce the objectives of the brainstorming session.
- Limit the session to an hour or so.
- Do not involve more than five or six people.
- Set the rules for how participants can interrupt each other.
- Listen.
- Accept all ideas that fit within the scope of the discussion, and aim to have contributors' ideas build upon each other.

------

[161] Surveys must offer a limited number of clear and unambiguous questions which call for facts and not opinions.

- Structure the brainstorming session into a few broad topics to be addressed successively (e.g., using a fishbone diagram[162]).
- Use walls and drawing boards to facilitate visual thinking and retain data and ideas for future sessions. Possible ways of organizing thoughts include affinity diagrams[163] and mind maps[164].

Lastly, crowdsourcing is yet another method to generate ideas for new product or service offerings. This approach solicits individuals or groups who are not necessarily stakeholders of the firm for the purpose of assisting with coining new concepts, solving a certain problem, or improving an existing offering. Firms may interest contributors in the process by affording them the possibility of gaining recognition, bringing their ideas to life through the firm's capabilities, or obtaining a financial reward, amongst other ways. Examples of crowdsourcing include having readers correct grammatical errors in a text or running a contest in which customers propose

---

[162] See chapter on Operations Management.

[163] Grouping related ideas under various categories for easier root cause analysis. For example, in a brainstorming session relating to a construction project, categories may include: design, safety, legal compliance, etc. Affinity diagrams are helpful to identify gaps in the thinking process as clustered data can make it easier to spot missing categories.

[164] Mind maps can be considered as a variation of affinity diagrams where a concept, goal, or idea is placed in the center of the diagram and related categories with their own sub ideas radiate from the center. Use of different colors, fonts, symbols, etc. can help enhance the clarity of such diagrams.

a t-shirt design, with an incentive of certain designs becoming a commercial offering.

Value Capture

Marketers must dedicate efforts into positioning the product or service in a compelling manner that resonates with target consumers. This requires finding methods to reach and service the right customers, in the right markets, through the right channels, with the right products and services and value proposition. One framework used to achieve these objectives is the so called four Ps, product, place, promotion, and price (also known as the marketing mix). Business plans are also used to structure the offering and add further details to the 4Ps[165].

The marketing mix or 4Ps			
Product	Place	Promotion	Price

Defining a value proposition

Product

A product or service is an offering that satisfies a need. Its attributes involve core order qualifiers that attract the consumers' interest in the offering, followed by features that consumers expect in the specific category of product or service, and finally, differentiators (order winners) that help distinguish

---

[165] First introduced by Market Vantage, a Boston based Internet marketing agency, the so called 4Cs, content, commerce, customer care, and conversion of Internet user visits to actual purchases is a recent concept that somewhat adapts the 4Ps to Internet marketing.

the offering from that of competitors.

Marketers aim to craft a product or service that brings compelling benefits to customers at an attractive price. This exercise is performed within the competitive context in which the offering falls by listing so called points of parity and points of differentiation versus substitute offerings.

Points of parity need to be tailored so that target customers believe the offering is at par with that of competitors and is worthy of consideration, while points of differentiation distinguish the offering from other products and services. These comparisons can pertain to the aspects listed below[166].

Once a product or service concept starts to take form, it can be useful to construct a prototype or implement a pilot project. Prototyping is an expeditious way to perceive the end result, spot immediate improvement options or inherent flaws in the idea, as well as solicit potential customers for their opinions. The iterative process of prototyping and analyzing can rapidly eliminate bad concepts or features and achieve the desired results.

Lastly, products and services are often offered in various colors and styles (e.g., gold, silver, or bronze) that provide more or less features, flexibility, and other differentiating aspects. While consumers appreciate some degree of variety in the offering, too many choices can become overwhelming and counterproductive. Marketers must therefore limit the

---

[166] See the chapter on Operations Management.

options in order to facilitate the sale.

Criteria
Ordering process: Lead time[167] and ease of placing an order.
Performance: Behavior of the offering in terms of its primary function.
Features: Attributes that enhance the perceived value of the product or service.
Conformance: Correspondence of the product or service to its intended specifications.
Learning curve: Time required for learning how to use the product or service.
Reliability: Ability not to fail.
Durability: Length of time the product or service remains reliable.
Perceived quality: Customers' opinions of the offering's quality.
Serviceability: Speed of repairing defects and customer service quality.
Aesthetics: Look and feel.

Comparison criteria of offerings versus competitors'

Place

The place refers to where and how the product is sold (e.g., physical store, online commerce), what the marketing (or distribution) channels are, and proper positioning versus modes through which competitors distribute their offerings.

Marketing channels are the mechanisms a firm uses to deliver its products or services to target customers

---

[167] Delivery time after an order is placed.

(stores, mail order, e-commerce, etc.). This can be accomplished through direct sales or intermediaries such as distributors, wholesalers, and retailers. The main benefits of engaging third parties in the marketing process include leveraging external market knowledge, sales power, and promotion networks. It is not uncommon for firms to use different channels for reaching various markets and segments, particularly in regard to international sales. In fact, partners with a strong local presence and knowledge of particular markets can be particularly beneficial. Factors for determining a distribution channel strategy include:

- Delivery times.
- Expertise for installing and maintaining the product or service.
- Market knowledge and existing market presence of intermediaries.
- Geographic complexity.
- Regulations (e.g., countries that dictate foreign firms take on local partners).
- Compatibility amongst various stakeholders along the distribution chain.

Promotion

Promotion refers to how target segments are made aware of the offering (e.g., advertisement campaigns, contests). Competitors' promotion strategies must also be taken into account. Communication vehicles of a promotion campaign can include[168]:

---

[168] A typical rule of thumb ("rule of seven") in advertising is that a given consumer will need to be exposed to the marketing message at least seven times in order to take

- Internet (websites, email, social networks, and blogs).
- Telemarketing.
- Personal sales.
- Catalogues.
- Mail.
- Newspapers and magazines.
- Television.
- Radio.

A good part of promotional efforts involve mass communication that targets large segments as a whole, with the aim of capturing the attention and interest of existing and potential customers. Personal communication is increasingly becoming part of these efforts as a means of tailoring the message at the individual level based on an analysis of large sets of data collected in a variety of ways (e.g., loyalty programs, online behavioral tracking[169], or customer surveys). Using this data, marketers create personal profiles and incorporate various technologies and methods (e.g. mail coupons, online ads) to push targeted promotional messages.

Price

Product and service pricing is not a trivial task and depends on a variety of factors such as a firm's pricing

---

action and place an order. The fact of the matter is that marketing campaigns are to be viewed as a continuous process, not a one-time initiative.

[169] The use of computer technology (e.g., tracking software, web cookies) to build consumer profiles based on age group, purchase preferences, etc.

strategy, revenue requirements, market demand and price sensitivity, competitor pricing, and regulations. Before setting prices, marketers and product managers will need to perform a profit and loss net present value (NPV[170]) analysis to establish a baseline for their pricing strategy, which includes an estimate of production costs[171], sales volumes projections[172], and pricing values. The NPV analysis will provide a framework for examining how variations of price and sales volumes parameters will impact the firm's profits.

Sales volume, or demand, projections rely on past data, external expert opinions, customer feedback, and the predictions of internal firm experts. Past data can be deduced from assessing the performance of similar products in reasonably comparable markets by examining third party market research or data collected on similar firm offerings. Expert opinions can leverage focus groups to make qualitative assessments of performance metrics such as expected demand for a given offering[173]. In addition, marketers can ask internal stakeholders, such as sales or customer support staff, for their thoughts as well as query customers directly through surveys. Regardless

---

[170] See the chapter on Corporate Finance.

[171] As obtained from various internal stakeholders who contribute to building the product or delivering the service.

[172] Stemming from past data, comparative analysis with competitors, customer feedback, and so on.

[173] E.g., Delphi method which relies on a panel of experts answering questionnaires in several rounds. Results from each round are shared with the panel, thus allowing participants to review their opinion, and ultimately converging to a common conclusion.

of how predictions are collected, demand forecasting will eventually come down to a quantitative estimation and a thorough examination of numbers or ranges.

With past data at hand, marketers can apply the moving average method to predict a future value (n+1) using the previous n values. For example, one may estimate the sales volume for the month of May using recorded values for February, March, and April and predict June's performance using numbers for March, April, and May[174]. Regression models can also be applied to existing sets of data in order to make predictions about future performance[175].

Another approach is the so called chain ratio analysis, which is a top down estimation technique that drills down the estimated performance of a specific offering in a particular market by making informed assumptions (e.g., using expert opinions as described above) about various calculation factors. For example, to estimate the demand for a new printer device, marketers may develop a formula similar to the following:

(demand for new printer) = (total number of target PC owners) ×
(proportion of printer owners) ×
(projected market penetration)

This formula can be improved by introducing projected variation rates for each factor or breaking

---

[174] A slight modification of this approach is the so called weighted moving average in which past values are given varying weights based on perceived reliability or relevance.
[175] See the chapter on Quantitative Analysis.

down the target market into more than one segment in order to improve precision (a method also known as market build-up).

Regardless of the estimates reached, it is always sensible to perform sensitivity analyses as well as simulations to vary multiple factors simultaneously and determine best and worst case scenarios. It is also useful to calculate break even sales volumes.

Break even sales volumes attempt to find the minimum sales volume beyond which the firm will make a profit. This involves listing fixed costs, those that must be paid regardless of sales, and variable costs, those incurred upon a sale. For example, a store's rent and utilities constitute fixed costs, while product packaging and shipment fees are variable costs that are not incurred unless a customer places an order. The profit equation is:

$$profits = (volume\ of\ units\ sold) \times [(price\ per\ unit) - (variable\ cost\ per\ unit)] - (fixed\ costs)$$

The break even volume of units sold is where profit becomes positive, in other words:

$$(breakeven\ volume) = \frac{(fixed\ costs)}{[(price\ per\ unit) - (variable\ cost\ per\ unit)]}$$

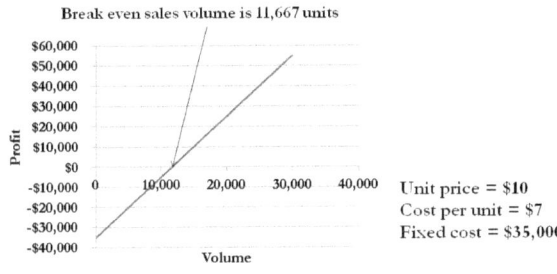

Profit = *(Total revenue) – (Total cost)*
= *(Price × Volume) – [(Fixed cost) + (Volume) × (Per unit cost)]*

Example of a Break Even Profit-volume Analysis

While pricing strategies begin with the analyses described above, they often look beyond cost of production and sales volumes. In other words, they are not solely focused on the firm's internal constraints. External factors also have to be taken into consideration, namely competitors and consumers.

Marketers will need to monitor and at times react to competitors' pricing strategies, depending on how they change over time.

As for consumers, they will compare offerings from various vendors based on the perceived differential advantages, which stem from the customer's perceived value of the benefits an offering brings versus its corresponding cost of purchase. The value equation captures this concept[176]:

---

[176] Note that price is not only material but can also be physical (difficulty of access), cognitive (complexity of choice), and emotional (familiarity with previous product).

$$value = \frac{(perceived\ benefits)}{price}$$

Increasing customers' perceived value can therefore be achieved by lowering pricing, increasing perceived benefits, or both.

In addition to a firm's internal constraints, which include cost of production and estimated sales volumes, the competitors' pricing, and consumers' perceived value, there are additional aspects that can impact pricing which are briefly described below.

Pricing may differ based on geographic location due to cost differences relating to transportation, labor, and commercial permits. Differences may also stem from variations in price sensitivities and the disposable incomes of target markets.

Firms may decide to intentionally lower their prices when an offering is first launched in order to gain customer adoption. This can prove to be a risky strategy as raising prices is almost always a challenge.

It is also possible for firms to intentionally raise prices beyond a reasonable profit margin in order to position the offering in a luxury category or achieve high profits from early adopters[177].

Finally, firms should avoid so called fake profits by

---

[177] Certain groups of customers often buy products as soon as they are launched, even at high prices. A typical example involves technology enthusiasts.

taxing consumers for noncore services, such as refunds or fees for setting up a customer account.

Business Plans

A business plan is a detailed explanation of a business project or venture in terms of objectives, approaches, projected gains, and other relevant components.

Consequently, business plans can be used to describe a new company or business unit, and sections, if not the entire plan, can be beneficial in structuring a product or service's value proposition. Below is a short outline of a typical business plan:

- Executive summary:
  o Enthusiastic description of the envisioned company or venture, explaining the who, what, and why of the project or business in a manner that sparks the interest of the reader.
  o Brief and concise (e.g., less than 2 pages).
- Business description and vision:
  o Mission statement (business purpose).
  o Business goals and objectives.
  o Company's growth and potential.
  o Brief history of the business.
  o List of key company officers and/or partners.
- Definition of the market:
  o General industry conditions (macro level view, market size, and growth perspectives).
  o Industry dynamics (trends, drivers,

obstacles).
- o Target customers (segmentation[178,179], perceived needs).
- o Competitive landscape.
- o Anticipated market share.
- Description of the product or service:
  - o Features and benefits.
  - o Competitive advantages.
  - o Technologies involved.
- Envisioned organization and management:
  - o Organizational flow chart.
  - o Legal structure.
  - o Relevant licenses and permits.
  - o Intellectual property.
  - o Biography of key managers.
  - o Recruitment policy.
- Operations:
  - o Premises.
  - o Assembly.
  - o Procurement.
  - o Order placement.

---

[178] Consumer segmentation is the process of dividing the market into smaller groups with similar needs so that each group will respond in similar ways to marketing initiatives. Segmentation can be based on demographics (gender, age), motivations, geographic locations, culture, race, nationality, behavior and buying decisions, needs, possible uses of the product, price sensitivity, education level, or income level.
[179] Market segments that are worthy of consideration must be measureable, accessible, and actionable. Measurable means one can estimate the number of customers in the segment; accessible means that the firm is capable of reaching the targets through promotion, distribution, etc.; and actionable means that the firm has the resources to offer a product or service that the segment needs.

- o Delivery.
- ▪ Sales and marketing strategy:
  - o Pricing.
  - o Promotion (advertisements, distribution channels).
  - o Place.
- ▪ Financial projections[180]:
  - o Projected profit and loss.
  - o Projected cash flow.
  - o Projected balance sheet.
  - o Sensitivity analyses[181].

Product and Service Portfolio Management

Product and service portfolio management relates to strategic decisions about allocating resources within the organization that will be used to develop and maintain certain products or services.

In addition to the financial analysis[182] of various projects, managers can map the attractiveness of business sectors versus the organization's competitive position. The objective is to balance the portfolio and invest resources in an optimal manner.

A balanced portfolio will have a product mix that provides income for present operations, funds for future high revenue opportunities, as well as room for riskier but potentially highly rewarding opportunities.

---

[180] Typically three to five years.
[181] Worst and best case scenarios as well as variation of parameters to observe the result.
[182] E.g., NPV calculation and data modeling. See the chapter on Corporate Finance.

The McKinsey-GE matrix for portfolio management[183] (pictured below) is one of the most effective methods for determining how to allocate a firm's resources and deciding on the primary focus areas.

Strength of the organization:
• Relative market share
• Brand strength
• Technology and R&D

		High	Medium	Low
	High	Ⓐ	Ⓐ	Ⓒ
Attractiveness of the sector: • Market growth rate • Market size • Profit margins	Medium	Ⓐ	Ⓒ	Ⓓ
	Low	Ⓑ	Ⓒ	Ⓓ

Ⓐ Invest to grow market share
Ⓑ Invest selectively to grow market share in certain markets
Ⓒ Manage costs and revenues to optimize profits
Ⓓ Optimize profits on the short-term, then get out

McKinsey-GE matrix for portfolio management

The Boston Consulting Group developed a framework similar to the McKinsey-GE matrix, which focuses on market growth (as an indicator of sector attractiveness) and the firm's relative market share (as an indicator of the firm's strength in the sector).

---

[183] Developed by the consulting firm McKinsey for General Electric in the seventies.

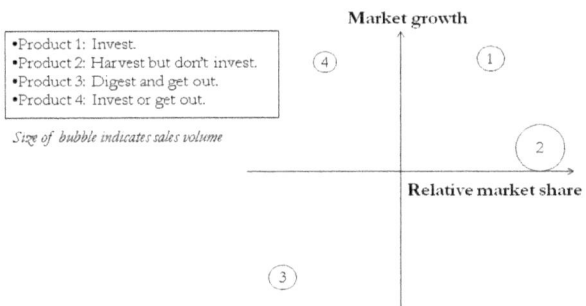

A simplified view of the BCG matrix[184]

When managing the portfolio, managers should pay close attention to achieving the right balance between the strategic focus of the firm's product line and allowing enough flexibility to reconfigure activities swiftly in response to market changes.

Another tradeoff to consider is the impact of new product or service releases on existing offerings, mostly in terms of sales volumes. When a new offering eats away at the market share of a previous release, it is referred to as product cannibalization.

Occasionally, some firms intentionally trigger cannibalization in order to stay on top of their respective market. Although a firm may sacrifice an existing offering's remaining profit potential, they prevent competitors from launching a new product or service that will eat away at those same profits.

---

[184] Developed by the consulting firm The Boston Consulting Group in the seventies.

Brand Management

A brand is one or more items that serve as a distinguishing symbol of an offering by a person, group, or organization. Icons, names, logos, graphics, and other images fall under the definition of a brand for a given entity.

Brands can be useful in rapidly identifying a product or service in terms of category, quality level, innovation, and trendiness. This section explores the following topics:

- Building brand equity.
- Measuring brand equity.
- Maintaining the brand.

Building Brand Equity

Building brand equity is not a fast process; it may take as a long as a few years. At the core of brand growth is the positioning strategy that marketers adopt. This necessitates a definition of the offering and image that the brand will evoke in the minds of target market segments.

Proper marketing communication methods aim at building the brand by associating it with the offerings it represents, the benefits those offerings afford, and how they are better than those of competitors.

Marketers must focus on positive marketing strategies that reinforce the brand (e.g., message of an ad campaign needs to resonate well with target segments) as well as identify and remedy negative strategies that weaken it (e.g., bad publicity due to product failure).

Measuring Brand Equity

Branding a product or service creates added worth in terms of customers' perceived value of the offering. In fact, the brand's value can constitute a high percentage of a firm's market capitalization.

Brand value can be measured using a number of metrics. Companies assess the value of those metrics on a regular basis by examining brand aspects such as:

- Market share.
- Price relative to competitors'.
- Customer retention, loyalty, and brand awareness.
- Perceived brand quality and reputation.

Brand	Value ($m)	Brand/market cap
Apple	182,951	42%
IBM	115,985	49%
Google	107,857	40%
McDonald's	95,188	96%
Microsoft	76,651	33%
Coca-Cola	74,286	42%
Marlboro	73,612	48%
AT&T	68,870	34%
Verizon	49,151	35%
China Mobile	47,041	21%

Estimated brand value and percentage of firm capitalization of top world brands[185,186]

---

[185] http://www.millwardbrown.com/brandz/2012/Documents/2012_BrandZ_Top100_Chart.pdf
[186] https://www.google.com/finance

Maintaining the Brand

Brand maintenance is a continuous effort that can be accomplished using a variety of means such as:

- A focus on the positive associations of brand benefits and value in customers' minds.
- Constant attention to negative associations that may emerge, coupled with swift damage control measures such as:
  - o Fast response.
  - o Honesty in error recognition.
  - o Transparency in describing measures to prevent future reoccurrence.
  - o Awareness of new products, changes to existing ones, and the evolution of the competition[187].

---

[187] Using Porter's five forces analysis.

VI. ORGANIZATIONAL BEHAVIOR

"To improve is to change; to be perfect is to change often" – Winston Churchill

Organizational behavior studies how people behave inside and between organizations. It covers the ways in which they relate, manage, and collaborate with one another in their efforts to make decisions, reach objectives, and ultimately achieve firm growth. This chapter will cover:

- Vision and strategy of the firm.
- Culture and values.
- Management and decision making.
- Human capital management.
- Organizational change management.

Vision and Strategy of the Firm

Vision and strategy relate to the firm's intended direction, beliefs, and values. Strategy enables a company to surpass its competition and realize its vision (e.g., its business model, position in the market, ability to leverage its core competences, and resources, etc.).

A firm's vision is a core element that allows it to maintain its focus as well as inspire and attract employees who are excited about the stated objectives.

When deciding on a vision, managers must remember that it must:

- Fit with the firm's culture.
- Be realistically achievable given present and future firm capabilities.
- Answer questions such as:
    o Who the company is,
    o Where the company is going,
    o Why it is important, and
    o How progress will be measured.
- Involve and maintain buy in from most if not all stakeholders.
- Convey the vision to stakeholders, employees, and consumers in a brief, clear, and concise manner.

Culture and Values

Culture is the common ground created by values and beliefs that defines how people behave, and perform their jobs within a company. A simple and commonly known meaning of an organization's culture can be described as the systems and procedures that have been established as a means of getting things done in the firm. A firm's culture is of particular importance as it can impact employee appeal and turnover rate, performance, and retention, as well as the creative output of the firm, and its reputation, all of which affect profitability. There are a number of frameworks that aim to define and measure the components of organizational culture. In the subsections below, the following topics are discussed:

- Hofstede's cultural model.
- Edgar Schein's cultural model.
- Roger Harrison's cultural model.
- Other cultural models.

Hofstede's Cultural Model

Geert Hofstede's cultural model relates firm culture to individual behaviors by analyzing cultural behaviors on four dimensions:

- Individualism: The degree of focus on individual versus group achievements.
- Uncertainty avoidance: The degree of tolerance of uncertainties and ambiguities. In high uncertainty avoidance cultures, people tend to be more emotional and risk averse, while low uncertainty avoidance settings facilitate a more practical approach and a willingness to embrace change.
- Power distance: A low power distance entails a flatter organization, such as democratic or consultative structures, while a high power distance follows a more autocratic power scheme in which subordinates accept the authority of higher ranking individuals based on their own position in the power hierarchy.
- Masculinity versus femininity: Masculine cultures place a greater emphasis on traits such as competitiveness, ambition, and power; feminine cultures value interpersonal relationships and quality of life.

As an example of how Hofstede's framework is applied, the following table compares cultural dimensions (on a scale of 1 to 120) between the United Kingdom and Japan[188]:

---

[188] http://geert-hofstede.com/

Cultural dimension	United Kingdom	Japan
Power distance	35	54
Individualism	89	46
Masculinity/feminity	66	95
Uncertainty avoidance	35	92

Comparison of some cultural dimensions between the UK and Japan

Edgar Schein's Cultural Model

Edgar Schein's cultural model invokes three elements:

- Artifacts: Aspects of the firm that are readily visible or palpable such as the office layout, logos, the jargon used at work, etc.
- Values of the organization: Representations of the norms and beliefs that the firm holds and projects as its image.
- Basic assumptions: Unconscious or hidden ways of behavior that are only identifiable after a careful look at the firm and its employees.

Roger Harrison's Cultural Model

Roger Harrison's culture model[189] classifies organizations into four categories:

- Role culture or bureaucratic firms which present a structured division of specialties, responsibilities, and interaction between groups and departments via well established and sometimes rigid processes.
- Power culture firms in which the power and

---

[189] Adapted by Charles Handy.

control rest in the hands of a few key individuals.

- Task culture firms which build on a matrix of relatively small teams. Employees join together in an effort to deliver a certain project; once the goal is realized, they disband and form new teams.
- Person culture organizations where the focus is on each person. In this type of setup, most of the initiative and responsibility lies in the hands of individual persons who work alone or with occasional interaction and help from others.

Other Cultural Models

Below is a brief list of other frameworks used to define and measure cultural elements:

- Deal and Kennedy's model which builds on history, values and beliefs, rituals and ceremonies, stories, heroic figures, and the cultural network[190].
- Scholtz' model which describes the firm as more or less stable, reactive, expectant, empirical, and creative.
- O'Reilly, Chatman, and Caldwell's model defines a firm's cultural characteristics as innovative, detailed, goal driven, people centered, team orientated, stable, and aggressive.

Management and Decision Making

A management model is the set of processes and methods through which managers determine firm objectives, allocate resources for the project (human,

---

[190] The cultural network involves various employee types who informally create, spread, and interpret stories.

capital), and exercise leadership and authority in order to align and motivate employees to meet the targets. Management models are defined in official company policies and organizational structures but may also be apparent from the firm's culture and strategic orientation as well as the leadership traits of the firm's management executives. This section discusses the following topics:

- Organizational structures.
- Leadership.

Organizational Structures

Organizational structures refer to the hierarchy within a firm. Examples include[191]:

- Functional structure: Employees are organized into groups based on the function they perform (e.g., finance department, marketing department, etc.).
- Divisional structure: Employees are grouped according to the product they work on (e.g., construction division, automotive division, etc.). A variant of this structure is the product structure which categorizes employees according to the products they are assigned to.
- Geographic structure: Groups employees based on their locations.
- Matrix structure: Structures the firm according to functional and product aspects simultaneously.
- Flat structure: Entails little hierarchy and relies on the continuous creation and dissolution of project teams (common in startup environments).

---

[191] Many large firms combine two or more structures.

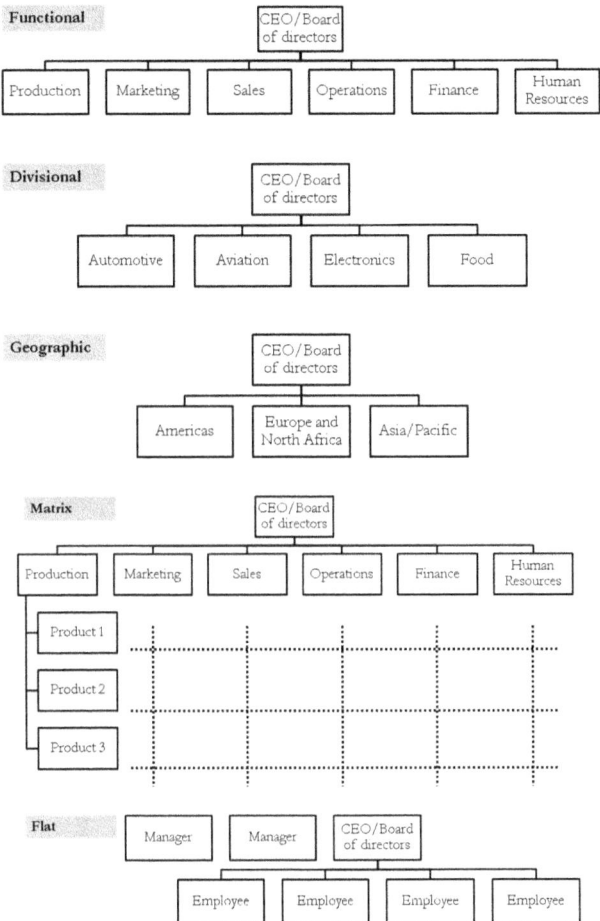

Illustration of various organizational structures

Leadership

Leadership is a key skill of an MBA holder. It involves setting a meaningful vision and direction to achieve that vision and establishing strong relationships with stakeholders and others in order to align resources and reach the goals. As such, leaders must pay attention both to people and tasks and keep an eye on the future while focusing on relevant details.

Many people prefer to be led, and as such will be ready to follow a leader who can establish communication with them, gain their trust, trigger their motivation, exhibit dependability, and infuse energy. Employees will also recognize the power in a leader in the form of one or more of the following:

- Legitimate power which is obtained by virtue of his or her function within an organization (e.g., a management position).
- Reward power which stems from the ability of an individual to award priced items such as pay raises, bonuses, or other benefits.
- Coercive power which derives from an individual's ability to inflict punishment (e.g., pay cut, termination).
- Expert power which emanates from an individual's knowledge in a certain field (e.g., medical doctor).
- Referent power develops from the respect and high opinion a group of people hold toward a certain individual.

A successful leader is approachable, easy to talk to, and able to use simple language while listening to others. Confident leaders value their critics and are not afraid to demonstrate vulnerability or admit when they are wrong. Trust is gained by maintaining respect, decency, transparency, integrity, and consistency with the subordinate. Leaders must keep in mind the importance of giving credit to others for their contributions instead of taking the credit themselves and not hesitate to dole out praise and encouragement as both can serve to promote and inspire creative growth. It is also crucial that close attention is given to what each person on the team needs at any point in time such as encouragement, space to perform, or emotional support. Finally, leaders must not postpone difficult decisions and take ownership of situations instead of pushing seemingly unmanageable responsibilities onto subordinates. In fact, perhaps one of the most common mistakes of an unsuccessful leader is to allow subordinates to become stuck between an impossible task and a demanding supervisor, a situation which can seriously undermine trust and motivation.

The insights described above constitute broad guidelines; researchers in the field of organizational behavior have devised a number of theories in an attempt to understand the mechanisms behind successful leadership, a few of which are described below.

Trait Theory of Leadership

The trait theory of leadership is perhaps one of the earliest attempts at analyzing the subject. It is based on the theory that certain people are born leaders and that leadership is rooted in innate personal characteristics such as dependability, ambition, and persistency. These three personal characteristics are now categorized into the so called Big Five personality traits: openness, conscientiousness, extraversion, agreeableness, and neuroticism. An alternative theory is behavioral leadership, which argues that individuals can adopt the characteristics that make a successful leader, and that leadership is more about what leaders can do rather than what traits they naturally possess.

Situational and Contingency Theories of Leadership

Alternatives of the trait leadership theory are the situational and contingency theories that assert that the environment and corresponding circumstances can create leaders, which implies that there is no single best approach to leadership and that conditional constraints dictate variations in leadership style.

Other Leadership Theories

Beyond examining individuals' leadership abilities, additional theories analyze the relationship between leaders and followers. For example, the participative leadership theory argues that leadership takes roots in the ability of leaders to engage others in the decision making process by seeking input from various stakeholders. Similarly, the transactional theory builds upon the management frameworks implemented by leaders which attempt to motivate followers through reward and punishment. Finally, the transformational leadership theory pertains to the ability of leaders to develop a vision and move it down the hierarchy in order to gain commitment throughout the entire firm.

Human Capital Management

A firm's human resource (HR) strategy is strongly focused on the management of human capital. Strategies differ depending on the firm's area of business, culture, and management preferences. Some firms place a high level of trust in their employees and in return, expect a high level of commitment from their workforce (e.g., technological environments). Other firms retain a low level of trust in their employees, who in turn exhibit a low level of commitment (e.g., high volume, low margin businesses). A successful human capital management strategy can be a strong competitive advantage[192] for a firm. In general, human capital management entails attracting, motivating, and retaining the right employees; it is about securing enough qualified individuals to carry out the firm's objectives. In this chapter, the following topics are discussed:

- Employee hiring.
- Employee performance.
- Employee retention.
- Downsizing.
- Groups and teams.

Employee Hiring

Recruitment is about finding the right person or persons for the job. This requires:

- Creating a proper job definition[193] that matches the firm's expectations.
- Maintaining a positive reputation among target candidates.
- Ensuring the candidates' suitability, not only in terms of skills and background, but also shared interest in the firm's objectives and compatibility

---

[192] A firm enjoys a competitive advantage over others when it has an ability or resource (e.g., proprietary technology, superior knowledge, access to better raw materials) that enables it to outperform competitors and earn more in a specific market.
[193] A proper job definition includes a title, background and skills required, duties and responsibilities, reporting structure, job location, travel requirements, work permit requirements (if applicable), as well as pay and benefits.

with the culture.
- Enriching the firm's human capital pool by maintaining some level of diversity in abilities (cognitive, physical, emotional, personality) and possibly demographics.
- Using an assessment method that corresponds with the job opening. If the role calls for a repetitive task with limited growth potential, exact skill sets and certifications are essential. If the position requires more creative output and long term growth, the firm must identify talent with long term growth potential. Candidate assessment methods can cover:
  o Discussions and chats with the candidate which explore his or her background, interests, and overall character.
  o Quizzes and riddles.
  o Situational interviews where candidates perform real tasks associated with the job in a team or on their own.
  o Aptitude tests or standardized test score results (e.g., GRE, or GMAT[194]).
  o Background checks (recommendations, credit checks, and criminal records).

If a new hire does not turn out to be a fit for the role he or she was recruited for, managers must do

---

[194] GRE stands for Graduate Record Examination and GMAT for Graduate Management Admission Test. Both are standardized tests that assess the candidate's English language skills and reasoning abilities. The GRE and GMAT are customarily used for graduate school admissions, although the GMAT is used more for business school admissions.

their best to discover what went wrong in the hiring process and ensure a smooth termination for the candidate by, for example, offering a severance package and assisting with job placement at an alternative firm. The reasons for gracefully parting ways are multiple and include preserving the firm's reputation and chances of finding other candidates in the future, not to mention that the hiring decision was probably more the firm's mistake than the employee's.

It is also worth noting that sometimes firms have difficulties finding the right candidates, given the available budget, time, geographic location, and other constraints. As a result, they may have no option but to choose from the available pool of candidates. However, this situation can be mitigated by allocating efforts into employee training and motivation.

An alternative method of hiring is to use recruiting agencies which assist firms find the right candidates. Recruiting agencies typically utilize two search models: the contingency search model and the retained search model. In the contingency search model, recruiting agencies propose a number of candidates which the firm commits to interview, and the agency is only paid if a candidate is hired. In the retained search model, the firm commits to exclusivity with the recruiting agency and generally pays an upfront fee regardless of whether a candidate is eventually hired or not.

Employee Performance

Adequate performance of the human work force is an essential factor in the successful delivery of a firm's strategy. Employees who perform below the capabilities they were hired for undermine the firm's financial performance both by adding to costs and taking away from revenues. As a result, employee performance is at the core of the organizational behavior field and the subject of numerous research studies, frameworks, and process implementations. Perhaps one of the simplest ways to examine the issue is by identifying the main employee performance drivers: motivation, ability, and opportunity. In other words:

$$performance = opportunity \times ability \times motivation$$

In the equation above, opportunity gives the employee a chance to perform. No matter how skilled or willing an individual may be, he or she cannot perform unless given a chance to do so. Ability refers to the capacity or talent that enables an employee to reach the goals set for a given task. It can be physical, cognitive, or emotional and can often be enhanced by training coupled with feedback.

Physical ability	Cognitive ability	Emotional ability
Usually cannot be fully addressed as it is an inherent limitation of the individual (e.g., weight that a worker can carry).	Intelligence and ability to absorb. It can be addressed to an extent through training and education.	Capacity to cope with one's own emotions as well as those of others. Of the three abilities, this is the one that employees can receive the most training on.

Three types of employee abilities

Finally, motivation is the subject of interest for many organizational behavior theories which tackle one or more of the following: personal needs, goal setting, rewards, transparency, and equity in dealing with employees. The next subsections discuss some of the most prevalent motivation theories.

Maslow's View on Motivation

One of the earliest motivation theories is Maslow's hierarchy of needs[195]. Maslow identified five levels of needs that motivate most individuals, beginning with basic necessities such as food, shelter, or physical security; followed by other requirements such as personal safety and belonging to a social group; and ending with recognition and intellectual achievement. The theory asserts that a person will not be able to take interest in higher level needs (intellectual) unless lower level needs are satisfied (food and shelter).

Theory X and Theory Y

Douglas Mcgregor's theory X and theory Y[196] are two motivational approaches that managers can adopt based on how they perceive the employees they manage. On one hand, theory X assumes that employees are naturally lazy and avoid exerting any effort, which translates into a need for managers to supervise and coerce them into working. On the other hand, theory Y builds on the assumption that employees are self-motivated and enjoy their work, which means that management structures must aim to create conditions in which employees can thrive.

Both theories have lost ground to the modern

---

[195] Maslow, Abraham H., and Frager, Robert. *Motivation and Personality*. New York: Harper and Row, 1987. Print.
[196] McGregor, Douglas, and Gershenfeld, Joel. *The Human Side of Enterprise*. New York: McGraw-Hill, 2006. Print.

approaches described below.

Expectancy Theory of Motivation

A popular analysis on motivation is Victor Vroom's expectancy theory. As illustrated below, this theory states that employees must first believe they have the ability to achieve, trust that the organization will reward them for their successful efforts, and finally, they must value the reward.

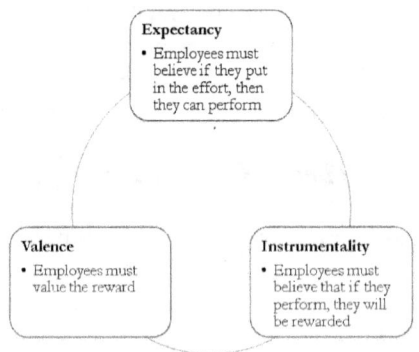

The expectancy theory of motivation

As a result, managers can assess employees' motivation by combining the three elements of the expectancy theory as follows:

$$motivation = expectancy \times instrumentality \times valence$$

Goal Setting Theory of Motivation

Another motivation management framework is the

goal setting theory which revolves around setting a specific, measurable, achievable, realistic, and time bound goal[197]. Implementation of this theory involves three components: agreement of employees and managers about the goals, acceptance by employees, and constant feedback from managers. This is referred to as management by objectives.

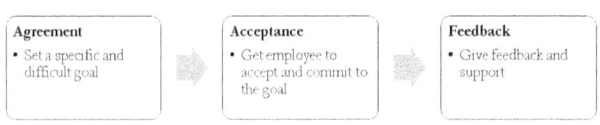

Agreement	Acceptance	Feedback
• Set a specific and difficult goal	• Get employee to accept and commit to the goal	• Give feedback and support

The goal setting theory of motivation

Managers can therefore assess employees' motivation as follows:

$$motivation = agreement \times acceptance \times feedback$$

The goal setting theory assumes that assigning challenging goals will enhance focus and motivate employees to deliver. In fact, some research indicates[198] that performance will increase up to the point in which employees become overwhelmed. Managers also need to keep an eye out for tunnel vision; employees often focus all their efforts on the goal at hand and ignore relevant items or tasks that fall outside the scope of the goal.

---

[197] This is referred to as the SMART framework.
[198] Based on the Yerkes-Dodson law. *See* Yerkes, RM, and Dodson, JD. "The Relation of Strengths of Stimulus to Rapidity of Habit-formation." *Journal of Comparative Neurology and Psychology* 18 (1908): 459-482.

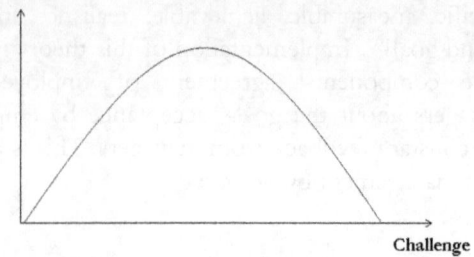

Performance versus goal challenge[199]

Equity Theory of Motivation

The equity theory is yet another analysis of motivation drivers which examines employees' perceptions of how fairly the firm treats them. Employees relate what they offer versus what they receive in return and become motivated if they feel the relationship is just; otherwise they lose motivation and occasionally retaliate[200].

What employees offer	Their expected rewards
Loyalty	Salary
Time	Benefits
Effort	Job security
Sacrifice	Career advancement
Ability	Responsibility

Example of employee contribution versus rewards

Employees will measure the factors above by

---

[199] Based on the Yerkes-Dodson law.
[200] Employees may reduce their performance levels, quit their jobs, talk negatively about the firm, or even perform acts of sabotage against the firm (e.g., delete files, destroy equipment).

comparing them with:

- Their own past experience in the firm.
- The working conditions of other employees in similar roles in the same firm.
- What they perceive the conditions may be for them in another firm or the working conditions of employees in similar roles in different firms.

The above comparisons assess equity using three components of justice:

- Distributive justice: Outcomes deemed fair by employees.
- Procedural justice: Process of deciding employee reward is fair. This requires managers to listen to the thoughts of their employees, provide explanations, and maintain proper communication channels between management and employees.
- Interactional justice: Employees treated with respect and dignity.

In short, employees' motivation will be based on perceived comparisons of their current contributions and the rewards, versus contributions to reward ratios in a variety of other instances, as described below:

Justice Type	Own situation	Own past	Colleagues' situation	Other firms
Distributive	D	A_1	B_1	C_1
Procedural	P	A_2	B_2	C_2
Interactional	I	A_3	B_3	C_3

Comparison of equity in treatment in reward to contribution for each of the 9 cases: D/A_1, D/B_1, D/C_1, P/A_2, P/B_2, P/C_2, I/A_3, I/B_3, and I/C_3

Summary of Motivation Theories

The theories described above are not necessarily to be taken as independent approaches to employee motivation. In fact, it may be possible to combine various theories, depending on work force characteristics, the firm's objectives, and company culture. In doing so, managers need to avoid common errors in performance management including:

- Not providing on-going feedback.
- Not providing clear performance objectives.
- Accommodating performance shortfalls.
- Using fear to motivate employees.
- Maintaining a high stress environment as a way to motivate employees - it will only work for a short time before employees burn out.

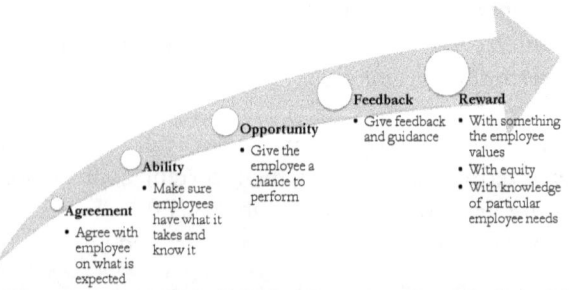

Combined view of motivation theories

Stress Management

It is no wonder that in a fast paced work place full of personality frictions and pressure to deliver, many employees are subject to more or less levels of stress. This can lead to a loss of motivation and absenteeism, which results in reduced profits. Managers must watch for signs of stress such as irritability, absenteeism, lack of interest or concentration, and high turnover rates, then quickly remedy the situation.

Category	Stress factor	Remediation option
Job	Employee's inability to perform tasks.	Training and fit of employee to position.
	Lack of direction and ambiguity toward objectives.	Provide clear and realistic goals that employee and manager agree on.
	Workloads (too much or too little) and time constraints.	Adjust workloads and deadlines and/or offer flexible work hours.
Career	Insufficient pay or growth perspectives.	Discuss with employee and be honest.
		Explore alternatives if there are no adequate growth options.
Relations	Difficult relations with managers and/or colleagues.	Social interaction (dinners, outings).
		Counseling.
		Training and penalties for harassment.
Company	Poor communication within the firm.	Allow employees to participate in the decision making process.
	Poor or untrustworthy leadership.	Management must be honest and consistent.
		Train managers.

Example of stress factors and remediation options

Employee Retention

Just as customers have a set of expectations upon purchasing a product, employees too have expectations upon entering into a work contract with a given company. To retain and motivate employees, managers must respect the explicit and implicit aspects of firm-employee contracts. The explicit part of a firm-employee contract contains details about salary, job title, role description, and other somewhat "quantifiable" aspects of the position. The implicit part includes unspoken expectations from both parties and is referred to as the psychological contract, the set of underlying assumptions each party has upon entering into the agreement.

The following is a list of some of the elements included in firm-employee contracts. While some contracts explicitly define the terms, others build on tacit assumptions or promises:

- Material:
  - Pay.
  - Promotions.
  - Bonuses.
- Personal:
  - Required working hours.
- Social:
  - Feeling part of the group.
  - Feeling appreciated (title, authority, popularity, etc.).

Downsizing

While retaining key employees is desirable, sometimes downsizing may be necessary; in such cases recommended approaches include:

- Proposing voluntary exit with bonus to certain employees.
- Proposing early retirement to certain employees.
- Adopting a "sweet and sour" approach in which the negative restructuring and downsizing effort is simultaneously alleviated by a positive set of parallel actions that serve to revitalize and renew the remaining work force.

Problems associated with downsizing include:

- Damage control for both departing employees and those staying behind (as a result of breaking the psychological contract).
- Disruption in motivation for remaining employees.
- Heavier workloads for remaining employees.

Groups and Teams

Although the terms "group" and "team" are often used interchangeably, experts sometimes distinguish between the two. Some definitions characterize a group as a set of individuals who work independently of one another and follow the direction of a leader, while a team is described as a more collaborative set of individuals with strong mutual accountability and shared responsibility. The group terminology can therefore apply to school teachers whose roles are independent of each other and who each report to a superior. However, when engineers in a software technology firm join together in an effort to build a certain product within the constraints of timeframes and objectives, they are more likely to be referred to as a team. In the remainder of this section, "group" and "team" will be used interchangeably, in reference to "team" as defined above.

Team Development Models

There are several theories that define the processes and steps behind group and team development, most of which identify an initial stage in which team members politely and cautiously "explore" one another followed by a conflict stage concerning role and power share before things stabilize and the team becomes productive.

The Tuckman model[201] is one of the earliest and most popular group development theories and suggests four stages in team building and functioning: forming, storming, norming, and performing[202]:

- During the forming stage, team members tend to avoid conflict and politely observe each other while discussing the project.
- The storming stage may bring tensions to the surface as people discuss tasks, preferences, and other aspects of the work; some members of the group will make a move for securing their preferred roles (e.g., leadership, research, etc.).
- If the team successfully moves past the storming stage, they will establish explicit and implicit agreements that define how things will operate within the team, referred to as the norming stage.
- With a framework for the modus operandi in place, the team will be poised to work and deliver in the performing stage.

---

[201] Developed by Bruce Tuckman.
[202] Several other models, such as Stewart Tubbs' and Aubrey Fisher's, identify similar steps.

Determining Team Structure

When assembling a team, managers need to consider the following:

- Team size: There is no "one-size-fits-all" when it comes to the number of team members. Size can vary depending on the field, skills required, amount of work, and project time frames. In addition, managers must be aware of coordination challenges as well as the need to maintain motivation and avoid "dead weight" on the team.
- Complementary attributes: Team members should complement each other in terms of skills, diversity, and personalities[203].
- Project definition: A solid description including a clear definition of goals and timeframes.
- Management: A healthy management approach will facilitate open communication, mutual trust, participative leadership, coaching and mutual support, a positive and optimistic atmosphere, and rapid detection and resolution of conflicts.

Conflict Management

Conflict can occur between individuals, organizations, governments, and any assembly of two or more parties coming into contact with one another. Disputes can be due to incompatibilities in personalities or objectives, scarcity of resources, lack of proper communication channels, racial or religious

---

[203] Personalities and psychological preferences can be explored using frameworks such as Myers-Briggs and the Belbin Team Inventory.

beliefs, different value sets, or other factors that lead to variances in preferences, goals, interests, or agendas. The discussion that follows focuses on team conflicts in the workplace.

Not every conflict is necessarily a bad thing. If well managed, a divergence of opinions can improve team performance and foster creativity, ultimately leading to increased profits for the firm. In his book, *There is an I in Team*[204], Mark de Rond argues that the long held belief that internal harmony must be established in order for a team to perform is now complemented by the notion that internal competition is equally as important in facilitating performance. He argues that the goal is to find the optimal balance between competition and harmony. On the other hand, unresolved or unchanneled conflicts can reduce employee motivation, raise stress levels, lower productivity, among other negative outcomes.

The goal for managers is to prevent personal conflict[205] while encouraging the discussion of ideas in a structured manner[206] that will harness individual team members' diversity and contribution into novel approaches and diffuse knowledge throughout the firm. Conflict management relies on proper resolution approaches and frameworks that serve to promote positive conflict. Several conflict resolution frameworks have been introduced, most of which

---

[204] De Rond, Mark. *There is an I in Team: What Elite Athletes and Coaches Really Know about High Performance*. Boston, Mass: Harvard Business Review Press, 2012. Print.
[205] Aka affective or relationship conflict.
[206] Aka substantive conflict.

recommend reducing emotional build up by turning the focus on the problem and away from the individual team members. This can be achieved by:

- Confronting stakeholders in a reassuring but fact based manner[207] and removing any fear concerning potential blame or retribution.
- Adopting a methodical and impartial problem solving approach that attempts to bring together valid and relevant points of various opinions.
- Forcing a certain course of action if one or more party is acting unreasonable or otherwise unwilling to reach a compromise.

Managers can also promote productive conflict by:

- Assembling a team of individuals who have complementary and conflicting beliefs and abilities rather than those with homogeneous minds and skill sets.
- Identifying and preventing groupthink, which is the unconscious avoidance of conflict even at the cost of following an erroneous course of action and/or making the wrong decisions[208]. With groupthink, team members may be happy with the

---

[207] See for example, Patterson, Kerry. *Crucial Confrontations: Tools for Resolving Broken Promises, Violated Expectations, and Bad Behavior.* New York: McGraw-Hill, 2005. Print.
[208] A similar pitfall is the so called Abilene Paradox which differs from groupthink in that team members consciously avoid confrontation thinking their opinion is contrary to that of the majority in the group. The result can be a group decision which none or most team members do not agree with.

group decision mostly because it gives them a sense of comfort knowing they share the same beliefs as their teammates and fit in to the group. The quickest methods for preventing groupthink are assigning at least one "devil's advocate" role to the team, soliciting external expert opinions, and assembling more than one team to work on the same problem independently from one another.

- Promoting a culture that embraces mistakes and turns them into learning opportunities rather than stigmatizing failure. This will encourage individuals and teams to defend their non- conforming opinions without the fear of censure.
- Turning the focus on ideas rather than individuals.

Finally, reaching a consensus can be attained by executing the following steps:

- Confirming all stakeholders understand the issues at hand.
- Listening to all points of view.
- Ensuring everyone accepts that a group decision must be reached, and that the decision must be accepted and committed to by all involved.

Organizational Change Management

Change management is the set of practices and processes used to enable transformation for individuals, groups of people, and organizations as a whole. Changes can pertain to a number of aspects including:

- Organization as a whole:
  - o Mission of the firm.
  - o Strategic orientation of the firm.
  - o Human capital.

- o Performance management.
- o Training.
- Processes:
  - o Customer relations.
  - o Internal communication.
  - o Project initiation and delivery.

Change can result from a number of reasons including:

- New technology.
- Changes in economic conditions, the market, laws, political conditions, etc.
- New management.
- New associations with outside entities due to a collaboration, joint venture, merger, or acquisition.
- Changes in competitor strategies.

There are a number of frameworks that guide change management efforts, most of which recommend setting a clear objective, engaging stakeholders, and continuously evaluating progress as well as effectiveness.

The change management effort can begin with a force field analysis, similar to the one illustrated below. The purpose of the analysis is to understand exactly what the future improved state is, contrast it with the current state, and identify which factors can facilitate the transition and which can stand in the way.

In terms of stakeholders, managers need to remember that reaction to change is inevitable and can be both positive and negative. Reaction can occur at several levels of the organization including organizational, departmental, and even individual. It is recommended to rely on trust when convincing others of the need for change and build teams of allies, particularly at the managerial level, as well as instill a sense of urgency in order to get things going. In the process, it will be imperative to maintain credibility, reliability, and consistency in describing objectives, benefits, and progress achieved. It will be equally important to use human resources processes and communication channels at all levels of the organization in order to stress the need for change, share the plan, and report on progress.

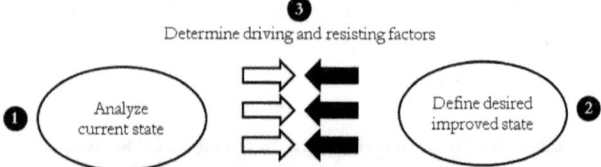

Force field analysis for change management

VII. OPERATIONS MANAGEMENT

"The ability to concentrate and to use time well is everything" –
Lee Iacocca

Operations management is the coordination of the firm's resources for the efficient output of products and services that meet customer demand. Operations management fuses concepts from management and industrial engineering and consolidates strategies, processes, and practices for the design and control of product manufacturing and service offerings. Because the management of production activities relates to the firm's overall strategy, operations management bridges the gap between the firm's capabilities and its strategic plans. This chapter will cover:

- Transformation processes.
- Operations planning.
- Process improvement.
- Quality control.

Transformation Processes

Operations is commonly described as the management of one or more transformation processes which turn one or more inputs into one or more outputs. Operations management is about the design, implementation, and improvement of the transformation process.

Transformation processes consist of a sequence of operations that use capital, labor, time, expertise, materials, technology, data, energy, etc., to create value in the form of products, services, or knowledge. Outputs can be tangible (e.g., car manufacturing companies) or intangible (e.g., transport companies that convey goods).

The elements of a transformation process are:

- Material flow (raw, finished, service parts, etc.).
- Information flow (orders, schedules, forecasts).
- Additional resources flow (money, people, expertise, etc.).

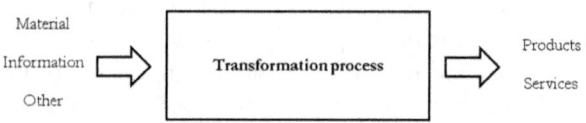

Illustration of the operations transformation process

Because firms generate products, services, or both, operations management addresses all the possible alternatives. As described below, there are key differences between the manufacture of products and services which affect how the firm delivers its offering.

Product operations refers to the production of tangible[209] items which typically require little to no customer contact. Those items may be perishable[210] or

---

[209] See the chapter on Accounting.
[210] Perishable items are those that decay in time when left as is, e.g., food.

non-perishable and the majority are able to be physically moved.

Service operations refer to the delivery of services, which are intangible[211] offerings which are perishable, cannot be physically moved, and typically require a high level of customer contact. One way to broadly distinguish services is to look at the degree of customization of the offering and the level of customer contact[212]. The higher (lower) customization and customer interaction, the more production efficiency decreases (increases) and cost of delivery increases (decreases).

Operations Planning

The transformation process described above brings together a collection of organizations, people, processes, technologies, and other aspects required to transform inputs, such as raw materials, into a finished product that satisfies customer demand. This set of interacting elements is referred to as a supply chain and builds on the production or transformation process and delivery mechanisms of finished goods to end users.

Making the various elements of a supply chain work together necessitates planning on a number of

---

[211] Not physical and thus cannot be inventoried.

[212] Roger W. Schmenner's service process matrix is a popular tool used to position service customization versus the degree of customer contact. (Schmenner, Robert W. "How Can Service Businesses Survive and Prosper?" Sloan Management Review 27.3 (Spring 1986): 25.)

levels including overall supply chain design, production capacity planning, and inventory management. The following subsections examine:

- Process design factors.
- Supply chain design.
- Production chain design.
- Inventory management.

Process Design Factors

Best practices recommend keeping customer needs at the center of operations process design. That being said, key dimensions to consider when studying a transformation process are commonly summarized using the four Vs of demand:

- Volume.
- Variety.
- Variation.
- Visibility.

Generally, firms either have low volume, high variety, high variation and high visibility (e.g., a professional services firm such as an architecture practice), or high volume, low variety, low variation, and low visibility (e.g., a utility company).

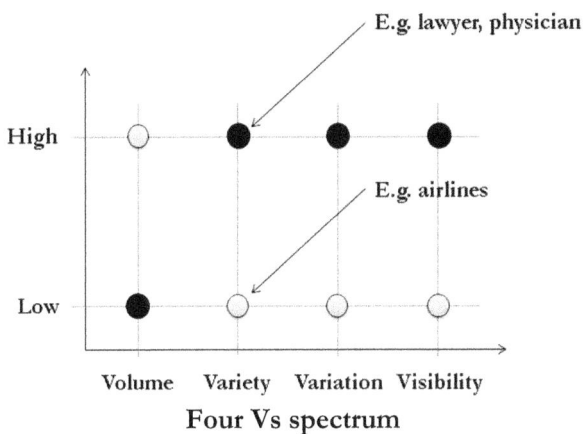

Four Vs spectrum

Volume

Volume is the level of a firm's output and is one of the strongest process design factors. Firms with high volumes usually adopt production chains which specialize labor into each subtask[213], repetitive tasks, and standardized outputs with little flexibility in customization, all of which lead to low unit costs for the resulting product or service. Firms with low volumes adopt somewhat of an opposite chain.

Variety

Variety pertains to the range of outputs offered by the firm (e.g., feature sets, product types, service levels, etc.). Similar to volume, variety is an important parameter in transformation process design. If a firm's

---

[213] E.g., producing sandwiches in a fast food chain with set menus involves a series of immutable tasks, each of which are performed by one or more employees who keep repeating the same action such as wrapping the sandwich.

offerings are widely varied, it will usually have low production volumes and vice-versa.

Variation

Variation relates to changes in demand for output types. If a company targets customers who need flexibility and adaptability in terms of when to place orders, variety in products and services, or customization of options, operations managers will need to plan for capacity and prepare resources accordingly. This leads to low specialization as workers will need to perform multiple non-repetitive tasks in order to meet the demand for non-standardized outputs, which leads to high unit costs.

Visibility

Visibility (or customer contact) refers to customers' ability to track their order through the production process. If a firm offers a high level of visibility to its customers, it will have to adopt advanced customer relations skills and give more personalized attention to customers so that the occurrence of a delay will not cause customers to look for another supplier.

Supply Chain Design

Supply chains can be quite complex and require careful design. Managers should incorporate parameters such as:

- Responsiveness, which is facilitated by:
  - Utilizing multiple production plants to allow for load balancing and flexibility.
- Security, which is enabled by:
  - Diversifying and expanding the base of local

suppliers.
- o Pursuing certifications (e.g., ISO, Honeywell, etc.).
- o Improving supplier and internal quality.
- Cost, which is improved by:
  - o Reducing raw material costs.
  - o Reducing processing costs.
  - o Reducing labor costs.
  - o Reducing waste.
- Sustainability, which is supported by:
  - o Reducing recycling waste.
  - o Reducing transportation pollutants.
- Resilience, which is enabled by:
  - o Protecting against strikes and natural disasters.
  - o Creating stronger linkages between various factories and business units.
- Innovation, which is fostered by:
  - o Capitalizing on core strengths of the firm.
  - o Performing incremental improvements.

Off shoring

Supply chains can span relatively large geographical distances between various constituents, such as the source of raw materials, production lines, and target consumer markets.

Off shoring is the relocation of supply chain components to remote or foreign locations due to a variety of reasons:

- Country specific advantages (CSA) which can reduce costs and include:
  - o Tax benefits.
  - o Cheaper labor.
  - o Better or more favorable regulations.

o Government subsidies[214].
- Access to talent pools in distant locations[215].
- Exposure to new practices and cultures which foster innovation.

The case for off shoring is usually reinforced by cheap transportation costs but is not without its own challenges. Many stress the importance of developing a customer base in the foreign market, rather than solely producing goods to ship back home, otherwise long term viability of the business case may be put at risk. Additional risk factors include:

- Reliability and commitment of international partners (requires clarity of objectives and an equitable relationship).
- Fluctuation in currency exchange rates.
- Protection of intellectual property[216].

Bullwhip Effect

Production managers often attempt to match output levels with demand. One essential reason for

---

[214] Some countries (e.g., Canada and the UK) offer R&D tax subsidies or low interest loans to encourage new ventures and foster economic growth. Such programs usually have minimal requirements and are relatively easy to take advantage of.

[215] E.g., a large number of multinational organizations maintain a presence in Silicon Valley, California in order to benefit from the specialized knowledge and talent located in that part of the world.

[216] Particularly relevant as the firm will relocate parts of its knowledge capital to remote locations that may have different legal environments and cultural frameworks.

this is to avoid unnecessary build-up of inventory, which freezes cash resources and can cause financial losses in the case of perishable items, technology obsolescence, etc. The question then becomes how to forecast demand with sufficient accuracy.

When multiple production units work in tandem to transform raw materials into finished products (which is the essence of a supply chain), each unit matches the demand for the following unit in the chain. Because the source of demand is on the consumers' end of the chain, each unit must vary its production level accordingly.

When improper information is propagated throughout the supply chain, changes in consumer demand levels can trigger wide variations in demand forecasts in each production unit along the chain. This is referred to as the bullwhip effect, which reflects the inventory management problem that can occur at each stage of a supply chain due to the difficulty in forecasting demand.

One of the most common methods of remedying the bullwhip effect is to disseminate information from distribution points interfacing with consumers all the way up to raw material suppliers. The use of information technology is particularly suited to address this need.

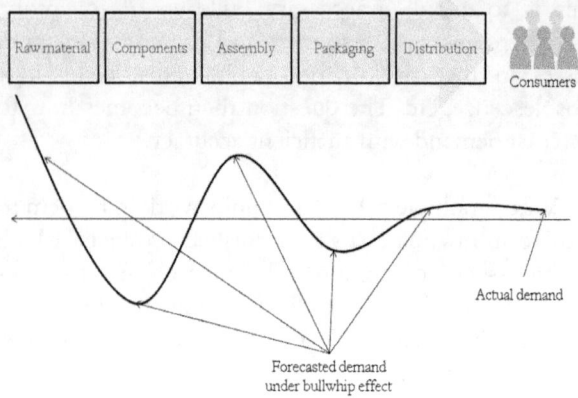

Illustration of the bullwhip effect

Production Chain Design

Production chain design focuses on ensuring the firm's transformation process is capable of efficiently meeting the demand for its products or services.

A transformation process can be broken down into a series of tasks, or production chain elements, as illustrated below.

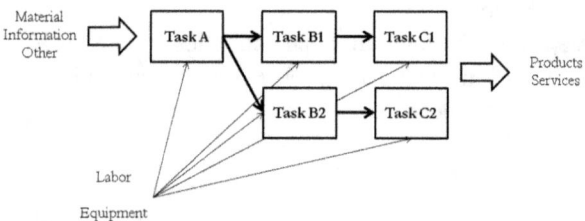

Transformation process as a series of tasks

Managers assign resources to each task such as labor and machines. Some tasks may occur on parallel production lines such as tasks (B1,B2) and (C1,C2) above. This speeds up the production process, albeit at the cost of assigning additional resources to create the parallel branch.

The production chain will output one or more product units at a time, but will not be able to take on more than its capacity or produce faster than its bottlenecks allow. Therefore, managers must keep certain performance metrics in mind when designing a transformation process, which are examined below.

Capacity is the maximum number of units that a system, such as a task or the chain, can produce over a certain period of time:

$$capacity = \frac{(max\ units)}{time}$$

Bottlenecks determine the overall performance of the chain which will be as fast as the slowest task. In other words, the bottleneck is determined by the task with minimum capacity, or maximum cycle time. The bottleneck task will cause units in progress to build up queues as they wait to be processed.

The throughput rate[217] reflects the actual speed of output of the entire production chain[218]:

$(throughput\ rate) = COGS = (capacity\ of\ bottleneck)$

Capacity utilization is the degree to which a task is

---

[217] Aka arrival rate.
[218] COGS are the cost of goods sold; see the chapter on Accounting.

being loaded with units to process:

$$(capacity\ utilization) = \frac{(capacity\ of\ bottleneck)}{(task\ capacity)}$$

The work in progress (WIP)[219] is the count of all units being worked on in the production chain[220]:

$$WIP = (total\ units\ in\ process) = (throughput\ rate) \times (cycle\ time)$$

Where cycle time is the average delay required for a unit to be produced by passing through every single task. The cycle time to produce an individual unit is therefore the sum of cycle times of all tasks on the production chain. For n tasks:

$$(cycle\ time) = \sum_{i=1}^{n} (cycle\ time)_i$$

The cycle time may differ from task time depending on the number of workers assigned to the task. Although the task time itself is fixed, adding workers may reduce the cycle time, at least to a certain degree[221].

---

[219] WIP is the inventories on balance sheets; see the chapter on Accounting.

[220] This is known as Little's law.

[221] Cycle time may decrease linearly with the first few additional workers; however, the decrease can slow down and eventually flatten out if new workers get in the way of existing ones.

Task	A	B	C	Total
Time (min)	12	20	10	42
Workers	1	2	2	5
Cycle time (min)[222]	12	10	5	27
Capacity (units/hr)	5	6	12	5
Capacity utilization	5/5= 100%	5/6= 83%	5/12= 41%	

Performance metrics of a simple process

For the simple process just described, it can be deduced that the bottleneck is task A, the process' cycle time is 27 minutes, the process capacity is 5 units/hr., and that:

$$(throughput\ rate) = COGS = 5\ units/hr = 0.083\ units/min$$

$$WIP = (throughput\ rate) \times (cycle\ time)$$
$$= 0.083\ units/min \times 27min$$
$$= 2.25\ units$$

To improve the production chain's performance, operations managers can:

- Align workers and equipment across the chain so bottlenecks can be addressed.
- Add labor and/or resources to various tasks.
- Outsource parts of the production effort.

---

[222] Assume cycle time decreases linearly with additional workers.

Inventory Management

Inventory is the set of finished goods, work in progress[223], and raw materials that a firm keeps in stock in order to:

- Meet future demands for new sales in terms of:
    - Lead times[224].
    - Volume of demand.
- Honor maintenance requests.
- Cut costs or make profits by:
    - Buying materials in bulk[225].
    - Taking advantage of product appreciation[226].

The benefits for holding inventory come with some limitations, mainly in terms of two types of cost:

- Purchasing costs:
    - Labor cost.
    - Transportation cost.
    - Insurance cost.
    - Setup cost.
- Carrying costs:
    - Cost of capital tied to inventory (and which can be invested somewhere else).
    - Storage cost.
    - Insurance cost.
    - Decay of perishable goods and materials.

---

[223] Unfinished goods which are in the process of production.
[224] The delays required to respond to a production request.
[225] Allows firms to achieve economies of scale.
[226] Future demand may rise and therefore bring prices up, while the cost of inventoried goods has been paid for.

o   Obsolescence[227].

Considering the tradeoff between costs and benefits, one can assume there is an optimal inventory size to hold. The Economic Order Quantity (EOQ) aims at determining this optimal value using the following assumptions[228]:

- The firm only purchases one item for its inventory.
- The firm's need for the item is known and remains stable throughout the time period under consideration.
- The price of the item the firm orders is fixed and no discounts apply with larger volume orders.
- The firm will order a batch of items at a time, deplete them, then order a new batch.

According to the EOQ model, the optimum size of inventory to hold corresponds to the size of each order to place because the assumption is that inventory will be completely depleted before each order. The order size Q is then given by:

$$Q = \sqrt{\frac{2 \times D \times C_o}{C_h}}$$

Where D is the demand for the item, C_o is the cost per order, and C_h is the holding cost per item in inventory.

---

[227] Refers to items that fall out of use, become unfashionable, or use outdated technologies.
[228] More complex models will be required when these assumptions are not applicable.

Say a company needs a fixed and known demand D of 50,000 units per year, and that the cost of placing each order C_o is $80.00, while the holding cost per unit C_h is 20% of the item's $2.00 unit price P_u. The optimal quantity Q to order is then:

$$Q = \sqrt{\frac{2 \times 50,000 \times 80}{0.2 \times 2}} = 4,472$$

Because the need is for 50,000 units per year, there will have to be 50,000/4,472=12 orders a year, each containing 4,472 units.

The total cost to the firm can be attained by calculating:

$$TC = P_u \times D + C_o \times \frac{D}{Q} + C_h \times \frac{Q}{2}$$

Where TC is the total cost, P_u is the unit price per item, D is the annual demand, C_o is the cost per order, C_h is the holding cost per unit, and Q is the optimum quantity to order per batch[229].

In the example above, the total cost will be $101,788. The graph below illustrates how the EOQ model results in the optimum value for total cost to the firm.

---

[229] The inventory size Q is divided by 2 simply to approximate an average number, as items will be consumed over time and will therefore not be held in inventory for the entire year.

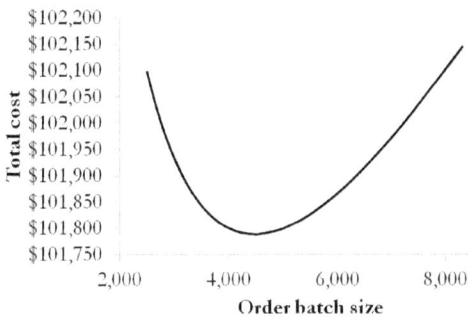

Optimal order batch size based on the EOQ model

Process Improvement

Much like any process, the transformation process can be improved on a continual basis, particularly as new technologies emerge, practices change, and labor skill sets evolve. Two popular process improvement frameworks are the lean and Six Sigma. Their core concept is that variation is the enemy of productivity; therefore both aim at removing variation[230] from the production process.

Lean

The principles of lean design are:

- Define what creates value for the customer.
- Identify steps to create value.
- Standardize work.
- Maintain continuous flows.

---

[230] Attributed to workers, machines, materials, and/or methods.

- Only make what is requested by customers, an approach referred to as Just In Time (JIT).
- Work towards perfection by constantly removing waste[231] and stopping to fix problems[232] as well as maintaining quality at the source[233] (i.e., do not let problems accumulate).

Waste refers to any unnecessary utilization of resources in terms of time or money. Build up of inventory, for example, is a waste as it incurs unnecessary costs of producing items that are not sold and depreciate while sitting in a warehouse.

A short list of wastes associated with product manufacturing include:

- Over production (this is the most critical).
- Excess inventory (which can hide several problems such as late suppliers or defective machines).
- Defects.
- Unnecessary physical movements (of workers, equipment, tools, etc.).
- Untapped employee creativity.
- Delays.

---

[231] Continuous improvement is an essential component of several production systems, particularly in chain assembly lines. The Toyota Production System relies on such continuous improvement, which is known as Kaizen in Japanese.
[232] Known as Andon in Japanese.
[233] Quality at the source is best as the cost of fixing a defect increases the further away the item moves from the point in the production line where it was introduced.

Wastes associated with delivering services include:

- Unnecessary physical movements (of workers, equipment, tools, etc.).
- Delay.
- Inefficient communication.
- Incorrect inventory.
- Lost opportunities to acquire more customers.
- Duplication of efforts.
- Errors in the service transaction.

Going back to the concept of JIT[234], which is a pillar of lean production, a steady flow approach, meaning one in which demand does not vary, is preferable. JIT calls for high visibility in the production process, which can be done, for example, by keeping all relevant information clearly on display in the production environment (e.g., dashboards in factories), and by maintaining open communication channels with suppliers in order to request stock replenishments when needed. Adoption of JIT almost always reduces lot sizes and inventory, sometimes by 50%.

Six Sigma

The purpose of Six Sigma quality management is to reduce defects and impurities in produced items by minimizing process variation. Six Sigma is customer focused in the sense that a defect is anything that does not conform to customer specifications.

Six Sigma's philosophy is that processes exhibit

---

[234] Known as Kanban in Japanese .

variation which can be measured, and with that information, variation can be reduced and processes improved. Six Sigma will therefore aim at increasing productivity by decreasing variation (i.e., achieving a continuous, smooth output flow) through data analysis (statistical process control and fishbone diagrams), reduced complexity, increased flexibility, and a focus on production lines of specialized outputs. In addition, Six Sigma attempts to eliminate waste by reducing employee movement (ready access to materials), removing bottlenecks, producing in parallel (as opposed to in a series), and producing in smaller batches. Six Sigma generally works best in large organizations and requires a significant amount of training. One implementation approach of Six Sigma is the so called DMAIC framework, which consists of:

- **D**efining improvement goal.
- **M**easuring current processes.
- **A**nalyzing issues.
- **I**mproving the measured processes.
- Implementing performance **C**hecks.

The Six Sigma improvement process aims to reduce the amount of defects to less than 3.4 per million units produced or services rendered. Sigma refers to the standard deviation[235] of process outcomes; Six Sigma strives for outcomes compliant with customer specifications within the zone defined by six standard deviations on each side of the mean.

---

[235] See the chapter on Quantitative Analysis.

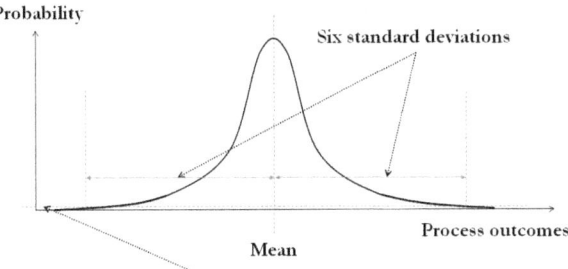

Illustration of the Six Sigma defect goal

Quality Control

There are various theories of product and service quality management regarding a firm's offerings. Many focus on the fitness of a product for a given purpose, as measured by customer satisfaction or conformance to pre-established requirements. The cost of ensuring quality is also relevant. Some argue that quality is free, in the sense that a firm which establishes a quality program will end up saving more than the cost of the program in the long run.

In reality, each firm has to find its own balance between cost of prevention and cost of repair. The first involves investments in processes, training, equipment, and other components that enhance the quality of the product or service. Cost of repair, on the other hand, is that of fixing issues in the product or service and is regarded as a damage control cost. Firms must seek optimal positioning between the two.

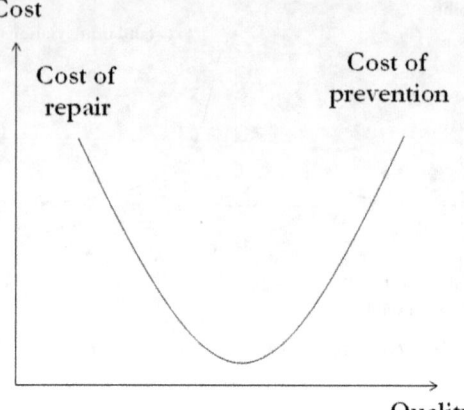

Cost of quality to the firm

Some of the tools of quality management include:

- Scatter diagrams.
- Pareto diagrams.
- Histograms.
- Check lists.
- Control charts.
- Cause and effect diagrams.
- Sampling.
- Task forces focused on improving quality.
- Quality training of staff.

As described in the chapter on Marketing, product and service quality can be measured with a number of factors. A firm does not need to meet all quality factors to satisfy customers and stay in business. In fact, it is practically impossible to exceed competitor performance on all fronts. To remain competitive, firms ought to exceed competitors' offerings on a few metrics and meet minimum acceptable levels on the rest.

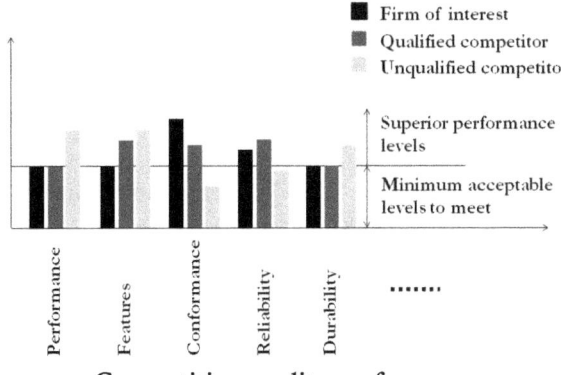

Competitive quality performance

Firms sometimes commit to delivering specified service quality levels to their customers. For example, a computer vendor will promise to fix any problems with its products within a certain number of days or hours of occurrence. In this case, firms offer so called Service Level Agreements (SLA), which can be based on target performance levels or Service Level Objectives (SLO) or guaranteed levels which are known as Service Level Guarantees (SLG). Guaranteed levels may be subject to penalties if the firm fails to deliver as agreed (e.g., monetary payments, rebates on future purchases, etc.).

Statistical Process Control (SPC)

Statistical process control (SPC) is a method of monitoring processes through control charts. One of the primary functions of SPC is measuring quality control[236]. SPC allows managers to monitor process

---

[236] Good quality reduces the costs of rework, waste, complaints, returns, and generates satisfied customers.

variations and trends in order to detect and understand the underlying reasons for changes as well as monitor the efficiency of any changes made to a process.

Control charts plot sample metrics relevant to the process (e.g., continuous values such as time, failure rate, weight, length, and cost or discrete values such as good/bad, yes/no, positive/negative, dead/alive) and also illustrate acceptable limits for satisfactory performance.

Typical control charts include:

- $\overline{X}$ chart: A line chart for a time series of means plus 3 straight lines for the average of means (which will correspond to the control line on chart), lower control limit (LCL), and upper control limit (UCL).
- R chart: A line chart for a time series of ranges plus 3 straight lines for the average of ranges, LCL, and UCL.
- P-chart: A line chart for a time series of proportions plus 3 straight lines for the average of proportions, LCL, and UCL.

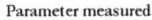

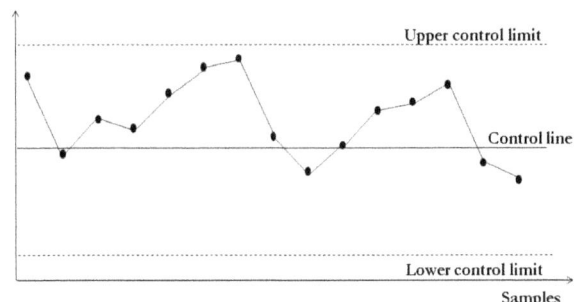

Illustration of $\overline{X}$, R, and p-charts

Constructing a $\overline{X}$ chart of n samples with a standard deviation s is achieved by:

- Calculating the mean $\overline{X}$ for each subgroup of samples.
- Calculating the average of the means, $\overline{\overline{X}}$, of all subgroups of samples.
- Calculating the standard deviation of all the data: s.
- Calculating the lower control limit LCL at the 1% significance level: $\overline{\overline{X}} - 3 \times \dfrac{s}{\sqrt{n}}$.
- Calculating the upper control limit UCL at the 1% significance level: $\overline{\overline{X}} + 3 \times \dfrac{s}{\sqrt{n}}$.
- Plotting a line chart for means over time.
- Plotting the averages of means, the LCL, and UCL on the same chart.

Constructing an R chart involves:

- Calculating the range: R = *(max - min)*, for each subgroup of samples.

- Calculating the average of ranges: $\overline{R}$.
- Calculating the lower control limit: $LCL = D3 \times \overline{R}$.
- Calculating the upper control limit: $UCL = D4 \times \overline{R}$.

Sample size	D3	D4
2	0	3.27
3	0	2.57
4	0	2.28
5	0	2.11

Values for D$_3$ and D$_4$

Constructing a p-chart is done by:

- Calculating the proportion for each subgroup of samples.
- Calculating the average of the proportions: $\overline{p}$.
- Calculating the lower control limit LCL at the 1% significance level: $\overline{p} - 3 \times \sqrt{\dfrac{\overline{p} \times (1 - \overline{p})}{n}}$.
- Calculating the upper control limit UCL at the 1% significance level: $\overline{p} + 3 \times \sqrt{\dfrac{\overline{p} \times (1 - \overline{p})}{n}}$.

Once the control charts are constructed, they can be used to check whether processes are exhibiting change patterns[237], as signaled by one or more of the

---

[237] E.g., due to human factors, material quality, process implementation, machines, the environment, etc.

following observations:

- Presence of outliers, with one or more points on the chart outside the upper or lower control limits.
- A shift in the process away from normal values, with a series of points in a row above or below the center line.
- A trend in the process, with several consecutive points moving in the same direction.
- A zigzag pattern, with successive points alternating up and down.

Charts can also be used to investigate whether changes are random or exhibit a certain pattern. Hypothesis testing is also helpful in determining whether processes are out of control or stabilized[238].

Once one or more issues are identified, managers can utilize several tools for process improvement, including both qualitative tools (flowcharts, brainstorming, or fishbone diagrams[239]) and quantitative tools (histograms, scatter plots, control charts themselves, or Pareto charts[240]).

---

[238] Hypothesis testing is a statistical method of testing a claim or theory about a given population based on a sample.
[239] A diagram used as a brainstorming tool in which team members are given the problem and several categories of possible causes to orient the discussion.
[240] Aka 80-20 rule or Pareto principle. Similar to an ordered bar chart but with bars arranged in decreasing order of frequency.

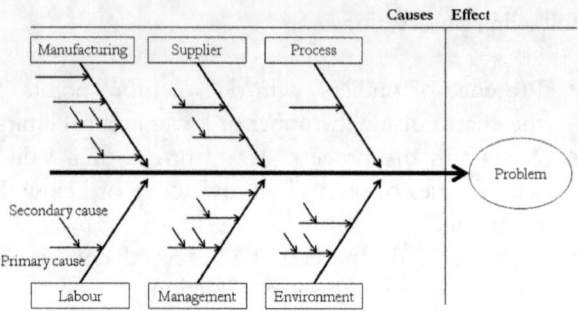

Illustration of a fishbone diagram[241]

_____

[241] First introduced by Kaoru Ishikawa.

VIII. QUANTITATIVE ANALYSIS

"It is a capital mistake to theorize before one has data" – Sir Arthur Conan Doyle

Quantitative analysis aims at converting data into information that can be used in decision making by applying mathematical, reasoning, and interpretation tools. It is a vast field, encompassing concepts such as probability, data modeling, simulations, and decision trees. This chapter will cover:

- Probability theory.
- Modeling.
- Decision making tools.

Probability Theory

Probability theory attempts to predict the likelihood of the occurrence of future events which can usually be linked to variables with a randomly changing value[242] or that follow a certain pattern. These variables may have a range of possible outcomes, with some more likely than others. This weighted view of potential outcomes is referred to as

---

[242] Meaning without apparent logic.

probability, which is the chance that a certain result or event will occur. Probabilities are expressed as a number ranging from 0 to 1.

Presenting Probabilities

A formal way of presenting probability data about random variables is to use descriptive statistics which include:

- The mean or average (denoted by μ), which is the weighted sum of all possible outcomes of a random variable with their corresponding probabilities.
- The median, which is the 50th percentile in the cumulative distribution function.
- The mode, which is the most likely value; the one that occurs the most.
- The range, which is the difference between the maximum and the minimum observed values.
- The standard deviation (denoted by σ), which is the average distance from the average for the outcomes of a given random variable[243].
- The variance, which is the square of the standard deviation.
- Percentiles, which represent the percentage of data below a certain value in a cumulative distribution

---

[243] For a bell shape, the 66%, 95%, and 99% rule applies, meaning there is a 66% chance that the result will roughly be one standard deviation from the mean (i.e. $1 \times \sigma$); a 95% chance that the result will roughly be within two standard deviations from the mean (i.e. $2 \times \sigma$); and a 99% chance that the result will roughly be within three standard deviations from the mean (i.e. $3 \times \sigma$).

function[244].

The mean, median, and mode indicate the typical behavior or overall tendency of a dataset. The other statistics show variability in the possible outcomes, and the extent of their dispersion.

Random variables with discrete[245] probability ranges can be represented on a bar chart (aka histogram). The range of values represent potential outcomes and bar heights indicate the probability associated with the occurrence of each of those outcomes. The sum of the probabilities of all possible outcomes must always add up to 1.

In addition, histograms illustrating the frequency of the occurrence of events can easily be turned into probability histograms by normalizing each frequency value by the sum of the frequencies of all outcomes. For example, if a group of 304 students is sampled in order to assess how many days it took them to finish reading a given text book, it can be observed that the fastest students took one day or less and the slowest ones took up to 30 days. A frequency histogram will show for each number of days between 1 and 30 how many students took that many days to finish reading the book. For example, 17 students took five days.

---

[244] Twenty-five percent is referred to as the lower quartile; 75% as the upper quartile; 25%-75% as the inter-quartile; P10 is the 10th percentile; and P90 is the 90th percentile.
[245] As opposed to continuous.

Example frequency histogram

To turn the frequency histogram above into a probability distribution histogram, simply divide each value associated with a given number of days by the total number of students observed (304 in this example). The result will show for each number of days the probability that a given student will need that many days to finish reading the book. The sum of all probabilities will be 100%.

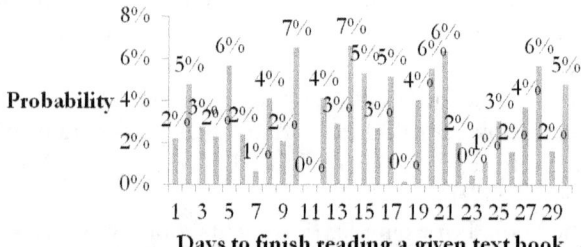

Probability distribution histogram of the example above

A somewhat equivalent representation of the histogram is a cumulative distribution function (CDF), which shows cumulative values of probabilities (as opposed to individual probabilities as in the case of histograms). The benefit of a CDF is that it determines the probability that an outcome will be less than or equal to a certain value. For example, there is a

60% probability that a given student will finish the book in 17 days or less.

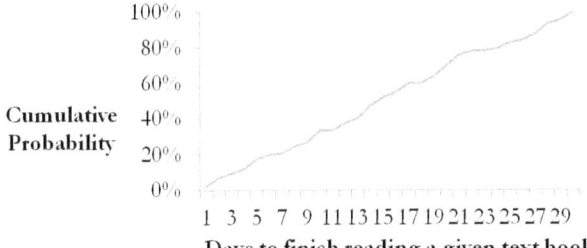

Cumulative distribution function of the example above

Random variables with linear probability ranges[246] can be represented on a distribution curve rather than a histogram, the most common of which is the bell shape[247]. Bell shapes are used in a number of disciplines to illustrate the probabilistic behavior of large populations[248]. A normal distribution is balanced around its mean, with the highest probability in that zone. Probability of the occurrence of events diminish symmetrically as one goes above or below the mean and hovers close to zero at a distance of 3 standard deviations from the mean or more.

---

[246] As opposed to discrete.
[247] Aka normal distribution.
[248] E.g., IQ statistics, disease statistics.

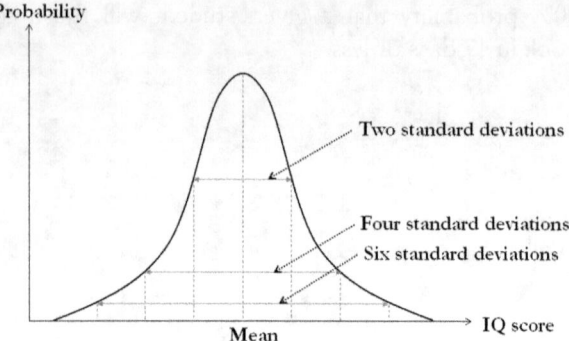

Illustration of a bell shape of IQ scores in a large population

Estimating Probabilities

There are several ways to estimate the probabilities of a random variable, which are examined in the following section.

Probability Estimation by Trials

One method of estimating probabilities is to look at the frequency of occurrence of a certain event as observed over a number of trials. In other words, run the event (e.g., tossing a coin) x number of times and identify the proportion of occurrence of the various outcomes. The more the event is performed, the more the percentage of data with a specific outcome will stabilize around a particular number, which can then be taken as the probability of occurrence of that outcome had the event been run once.

Probability Estimation by Opinion

Another way to determine probabilities is to seek expert, public, or market opinions. The Delphi method, for example, solicits the opinions of a group of experts and asks them to come to a common conclusion[249]. Probabilities in this case are a subjective measure of belief that an event will happen on a scale of 0 to 1.

Probability Estimation by Sampling

A sample is a subset of the population; by analyzing samples, managers can infer statistics about the population.

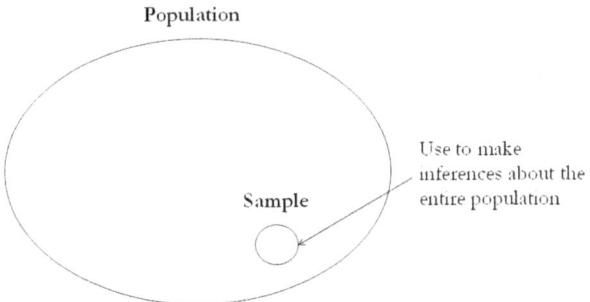

Population

Use to make inferences about the entire population

Sample

Illustration of sampling

It is usually safer to give range estimates as opposed to single values when trying to estimate population statistics. Confidence intervals are range estimates that are calculated based on a desired level of trust, or confidence, in that estimate. For example, a 95% confidence interval for the population's mean implies a 95% certainty that the population mean is within that interval. For a sample of size n, mean μ,

---

[249] A panel of experts answers questionnaires in several rounds. The results from each round are shared with the panel, thus allowing participants to review the opinions and ultimately agree on a conclusion.

and standard deviation σ, rough confidence intervals[250] for the population mean can be calculated as:

50% confidence interval:

$$[(\mu - 0.675 \times \frac{\sigma}{\sqrt{n}}); (\mu + 0.675 \times \frac{\sigma}{\sqrt{n}})]$$

68% confidence interval:

$$[(\mu - \frac{\sigma}{\sqrt{n}}); (\mu + \frac{\sigma}{\sqrt{n}})]$$

90% confidence interval:

$$[(\mu - 1.645 \times \frac{\sigma}{\sqrt{n}}); (\mu + 1.645 \times \frac{\sigma}{\sqrt{n}})]$$

95% confidence interval:

$$[(\mu - 1.96 \times \frac{\sigma}{\sqrt{n}}); (\mu + 1.96 \times \frac{\sigma}{\sqrt{n}})]$$

98% confidence interval:

$$[(\mu - 2.33 \times \frac{\sigma}{\sqrt{n}}); (\mu + 2.33 \times \frac{\sigma}{\sqrt{n}})]$$

99% confidence interval:

---

[250] There are two ways to reduce the width of confidence intervals: increase the sample size or reduce the confidence level.

$$[(\mu - 2.58 \times \frac{\sigma}{\sqrt{n}}); (\mu + 2.58 \times \frac{\sigma}{\sqrt{n}})]$$

Modeling

Modeling is the process of understanding the dynamics that govern the functions of a given process or system, then applying past data in order to analyze performance, identify opportunities for improvement, as well as make predictions about future behavior or outcomes. The modeling process entails:

- Model formulation.
- Analysis of the model.
- Data regressions.

Model Formulation

Model formulation will usually show that some outcomes depend on others through more or less complex equations. For example, a financial analysis will relate profit to revenues and cost, which in turn depend on other parameters such as price, sales volume, and fixed and variable costs. If profit is a key performance indicator (KPI), meaning a parameter of interest to managers, then it can be said that the other variables listed above constitute key performance drivers (KPDs) because the KPI of interest depends on them.

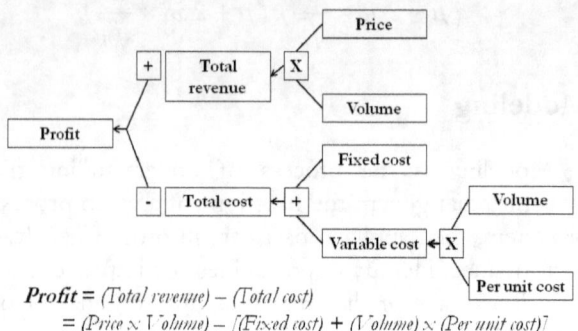

Profit = *(Total revenue) – (Total cost)*
= *(Price × Volume) – [(Fixed cost) + (Volume) × (Per unit cost)]*

Illustration of a simple model for profit analysis

Analysis of the Model

Once a model is in place, one can modify KPDs and observe outcomes. Computer simulations can perform several different calculations of possible values of one or more KPI by varying the underlying KPDs in accordance with their own probability distributions. This will give a statistical understanding of the dependent variable's possible outcomes.

To run a simulation, start with a model, as described above, then assign random variables values using functions that represent their respective probability distributions[251]. Each time the simulation is run, those functions pick a single value for every

---

[251] When assigning a probability distribution to a variable, one must make sure to adjust (i.e., subtract or add the difference) the average of the probability distribution with the known average of the variable. For example, if the probability distribution has an average X while the variable is known to have a variable Y, add to the probability function the difference between X and Y.

random variable, leading to one possible outcome for the result under investigation. Multiple simulation runs will therefore help produce a probability distribution for the result. In effect, simulations allow probability estimations by trials.

Consider the following model for profit, where:

- Price is a random variable with a normal distribution of mean $200 and standard deviation $50.00.
- Volume is a uniformly distributed variable with values between 500 and 3,000.
- Per unit variable cost is a random variable with a normal distribution of mean 0.6 and standard deviation 0.1.

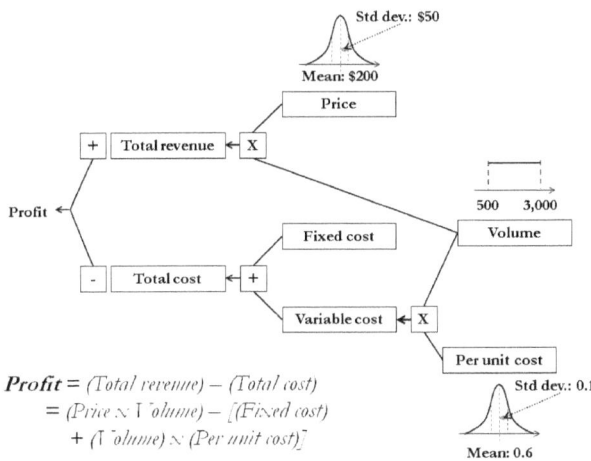

$Profit$ = (Total revenue) − (Total cost)
= (Price × Volume) − [(Fixed cost)
+ (Volume) × (Per unit cost)]

Profit analysis with variable driving parameters

A Monte Carlo simulation can calculate the value for profit resulting from a large number of possible values for each of the variable driving parameters (i.e., price, volume, and per unit variable cost). This can be done using a variety of software tools[252]. The result of the simulation will show the probability distribution of profit[253].

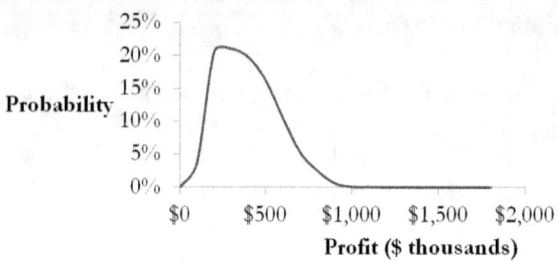

Probability distribution of profit with a computer simulation

Data Regressions

In many instances, the equations that govern a certain system are not easy to identify. One may have large amounts of data for variables that seem to relate to each other, but the relationships may remain unclear. In this case, data regression is a useful technique of formulating a model based on the data at hand.

Data regressions use past data to develop a model that can be used to predict future outcomes of a given variable. A simple data regression aims at finding a

---

[252] E.g., Microsoft Excel, IBM's SPSS, Oracle's Crystal Ball.
[253] Monte Carlo simulations are so named as an analogy to recording a large set of gambling results in a casino; Monte Carlo, Monaco is well known for its casinos.

linear[254] relation between two variables, a dependent variable Y, and an independent (aka driver) variable X. Given a certain data set, the regression will attempt to define the following relation:

$$Y = \beta_0 + \beta_1 \times X$$

Where β_0 and β_1 are constants, β_0 is the Y-intercept, meaning the value of Y where the line hits the vertical Y-axis, and β_1 is the slope or gradient of the line. Tools such as Data Analysis in Microsoft Excel[255] can be used to obtain estimates for the coefficients β in the equation.

The reliability of the model must be tested based on the statistical significance of the coefficients in the model's equation as well as the overall validity of the model. When performing data regression using Microsoft Excel, one must aim for:

- Small p-values[256], under 5% for each coefficient in the regression equation.
- Large t-stat values, over 2.
- A small standard error for each of the coefficients[257].

---

[254] Non-linear relations are also possible and sometimes more appropriate. Options include models that are exponential, logarithmic, trigonometric, etc.
[255] Typically requires the Analysis ToolPak.
[256] The p-value is the probability that a particular coefficient is zero. If that probability is small, the driving variable associated with that coefficient will explain changes in the dependent variable Y.
[257] Ignoring the intercept.

- A value for R^2 as close to 1 as possible but at least higher than 0.3. R^2 gives an indication of the extent to which changes in the dependent variable Y are due to changes in the independent variable X.

If coefficients of the model are not statistically satisfactory, one should try to improve them by omitting some outlier data[258] from the data set being fed into the regression analysis tool[259] as well as including different variables.

Multiple linear regression is similar to simple linear regression except that it relies on more than one driving variable. With n such variables, the model's equation can be written as:

$$Y = \beta_0 + \beta_1 \times X_1 + \beta_2 \times X_2 + ... + \beta_n \times X_n$$

An important aspect to watch out for with multiple regressions is multicollinearity, whereby driving variables have a high correlation amongst each other. Multicollinearity can be detected based on the correlation coefficients produced by Excel. If two variables have a high correlation, remove one of them and monitor the t-stat, p-value, and similar indicators of a good regression model.

---

[258] Data points that do not seem to fit with the rest.
[259] This approach must be used with care. Some outliers may in fact hide useful samples of possible outcomes, and excluding them will result in a less realistic model. Nicolas Taleb argues that such outliers – which he calls black swans – often hold the essence of a system's behavior (Taleb, Nassim N. *The Black Swan: The Impact of the Highly Improbable.* New York: Random House Trade Paperbacks, 2010. Print).

As an example, if one wanted to identify the driving factors behind movie revenue using data regression, one may suspect that production costs are a relevant driving parameter, while the relevancy of the production year is less certain. In order to come to a determination, a regression analysis can be applied that includes both production costs and production year.

Movie	Year	Cost	Revenue
Titanic	1997	$200m	$2,185m
Terminator 2	1991	$100m	$519m
Home Alone	1990	$18m	$476m
Rocky 4	1985	$28m	$300m
Independence Day	1996	$75m	$817m
Lord of the Rings 3	2003	$94m	$1,119m
Jurassic Park 1	1993	$63m	$914m
Toy Story	1995	$30m	$361m
Shrek	2001	$60m	$484m
Spiderman 2	2004	$200m	$783m
Superman Returns	2006	$209m	$404m
Dark Knight Rises	2012	$230m	$1,081m
Harry Potter 1	2001	$125m	$974m
Forrest Gump	1994	$55m	$677m
Avatar	2009	$237m	$2,782m
Star wars 3	2005	$113m	$848m

Sample of successful movies in the box office[260]

In this 95% confidence interval regression (as specified in the setting of the regression analysis in Microsoft Excel), observe the following:

---

[260] Dollar values are not adjusted for inflation.

Regression Statistics	
Multiple R	0.635705672
R Square	0.404121702
Adjusted R Square	0.312448117
Standard Error	555781184.3
Observations	16

Results	Intercept	β_1	β_2
Coefficients	2.579E+10	-1281451	6.519108
Standard Error	6.224E+10	3127809	3.056749
t-stat	0.414282	-0.409696	2.132692
p-value	0.6854218	0.688699	0.052590

Regression analysis[261] with Revenues versus Year and Costs

Remember to aim for the following values:

- Small p-values, under 5% for each coefficient.
- Large t-stat values, over 2.
- A small standard error for each of the coefficients[262].
- A value for R^2 or adjusted R^2 close to 1, and preferably above 0.3.

Although R^2 and adjusted R^2 have acceptable values, we see that the t-stat, p-value and standard error for the first variable (namely production year) are way off what we hope for. Although those for the second variable, i.e. production cost, have acceptable values, we must conclude that production year must

---

[261] Produced using the Data Analysis tool in Microsoft Excel 2007.
[262] Ignoring the intercept.

probably be excluded from the model since it does not drive movie revenues.

We therefore run the regression analysis again, this time with costs as the single variable. This time around, the t-stat and p-value for the costs variable have acceptable values as do R^2 (which tells us that nearly 39% of the variation in revenues is due to costs) and adjusted R^2. This model can be deemed useful and be defined by:

revenues = 285,661,125.1 + 5.531980059 × cos ts

Regression Statistics	
Multiple R	0.629625248
R Square	0.396427952
Adjusted R Square	0.353315663
Standard Error	539010559.3
Observations	16

Results	Intercept	β_1
Coefficients	285661125.1	5.53198005
Standard Error	249056533	1.82431157
t-stat	1.146973025	3.03236582
p-value	0.270617	0.00895

Result of the second regression attempt

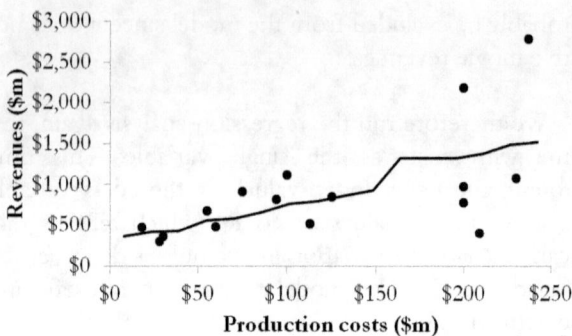

Plot of the regression equation versus the original data set

Extrapolation is not recommended when using regression models. In the above example, the range of production costs in the data set is $18m to $237m. It is therefore not recommended to use the model when predicting revenues that may result from costs that fall outside this range.

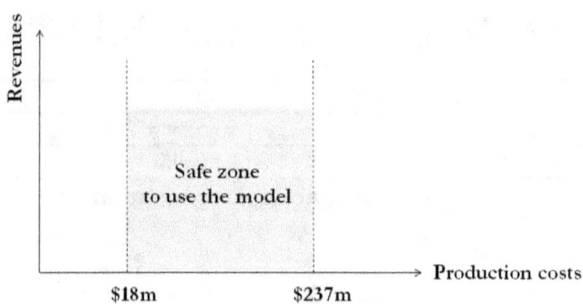

Safe zones to use our example model

Now assume that the production costs of a given movie are $45m. Because $45m is in the $18m to $237m range, the model above can be used to arrive at a point estimate of the revenues as follows:

$$revenues = 285,661,125.1 + 5.531980059 \times cos\ ts$$
$$= 285,661,125.1 + 5.531980059 \times 4,500,000$$
$$= 534,600,227$$

A point estimate of the revenues for this movie is therefore $534,600,227.

Decisions Making Tools

Business decision making requires data gathering, analysis, frameworks, and intuition. There are a large number of tools and approaches for decision making, two of which, decision trees and game theory, are discussed in the next subsections.

Decision Trees

Decision trees are used to determine the best course of action given uncertain outcomes because they place numerical values on those outcomes. Combined with probability information[263] about various possibilities and their consequences, decision trees can, for example, be used to analyze an investment portfolio, determine whether to build or buy, and devise the best operations strategy. Managers can build decision trees by:

- Choosing a decision to make.
- Identifying outcomes that can follow from a decision (usually based on past behavior).
- Assigning probabilities of occurrence and numerical values to each outcome.

---

[263] From analyses such as modeling or sampling.

With this data at hand, decision trees are built from left to right, starting with the desired decision to make, followed by the possibilities of achieving each outcome. Probabilities are associated with various possibilities as well as expected return or loss. Decision trees can have one of two types of nodes:

- Decision nodes, which are represented by a square.
- Chance nodes, represented by a circle. This is where different outcomes could occur.

Once relations between the tree's nodes are established, managers can run sensitivity analyses[264] to assess the effect of changing some values in the nodes (for probabilities or profit/cost) and even simulations to vary several such values simultaneously.

---

[264] Sensitivity analysis fixes the value of variable parameters except one of them (the sensitive variable), then calculates the outputs associated with several values of that sensitive variable over its possible range of variation. The output of sensitivity analyses can be illustrated in a tornado diagram, which is a vertical bar chart showing the impact of the variation of each parameter on the final output. Tornado diagrams are therefore useful to identify the parameters with the highest impact on the project.

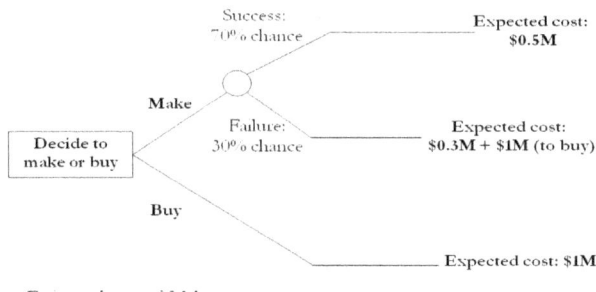

Estimated cost of Make:
$70\% \times \$0.5M + 30\% \times (\$0.3M + \$1M) = \$0.74M$

It therefore seems more advantageous to make than to buy. Note that we assume the project will stop before completion in case of failure.

Example decision tree for a make or buy decision

Game Theory

Game theory analyzes the decision making processes of players who plan their actions based on their own payoffs and what they estimate their opponents' to be in each possible outcome. Perhaps the most common example of game theory is the prisoner's dilemma. It is stated as follows[265]:

Two partner criminals are arrested and imprisoned. Each prisoner is in solitary confinement with no means of speaking to or exchanging messages with the other. The police offer each prisoner a bargain. If he betrays and testifies against his partner, while the latter stays silent, the first will go free while the partner will get three years in prison. If both prisoners betray and testify against each other, both will be sentenced to two years in jail. And if both stay silent and effectively

---

[265] Adapted from: Poundstone, W. *Prisoner's Dilemma*. New York, N.Y.: Doubleday, 1992. Print.

cooperate with one another, they will each get one year in jail.

		Prisoner 1	
		Stay silent	Betray
Prisoner 2	Stay silent	(1,1)	(0,3)
	Betray	(3,0)	(2,2)

Illustration of the prisoner's dilemma[266]

Based on the above, a game theoretical analysis will examine the best course of action for each prisoner. From the viewpoint of prisoner 1, assuming he stays silent, he will think that prisoner 2 is better off betraying him.

Again, from the viewpoint of prisoner 1, if he betrays his partner, then he will conclude that prisoner 2 is better off betraying him. As prisoner 2 will have the same reasoning, both prisoners (assuming they are rational individuals) will betray one another and each be sentenced to two years in jail.

In reality, both prisoners would have been better off cooperating with one another. However, because the game is played only once, the prisoners will not take a risk trusting the other will stay silent.

The prisoner's dilemma is a onetime run of a game theory problem. Other games may involve iterative steps of sequential decision making. In the long run, players may retaliate and cooperate until a state of equilibrium is reached. When each player in a game

---

[266] Sentences for prisoners are denoted by (x,y), where x is the jail term for prisoner 1 and y for prisoner 2.

theory problem chooses the best course of action available given the decisions of other players, the collective decisions of all players is referred to as Nash equilibrium

A repetitive prisoner's dilemma game illustrates this concept. In this case, each run of the game will add prison time to each player depending on the outcome of the round. For example, one of the prisoners may take a chance and trust the other. Should the opponent stay silent as well, they may keep on cooperating during each run of the game, thereby cumulating a minimal total of years in jail. However, if one of the prisoners betrays the other, then not only will the opponent probably lose trust, the betraying prisoner will also expect retaliation and therefore not trust the other. The result is a series of sub optimal outcomes for both. On a managerial decision making level, this example illustrates the difficulty of initially gaining trust and recovering it should it be lost.

Run	Prisoner 1	Prisoner 2	Result	Jail years
1	Cooperate	Cooperate	(1,1)	(1,1)
2	Cooperate	Cooperate	(1,1)	(2,2)
3	Cooperate	Cooperate	(1,1)	(3,3)
4	Cooperate	Cooperate	(1,1)	(4,4)

Repetitive prisoner's dilemma game with continuous mutual trust

Run	Prisoner 1	Prisoner 2	Result	Jail years
1	Cooperate	Betray	(3,0)	(3,0)
2	Betray	Cooperate	(0,3)	(3,3)
3	Betray	Betray	(2,2)	(5,5)
4	Betray	Betray	(2,2)	(7,7)

Repetitive prisoner's dilemma game with betrayal

Complex decision making problems can rely on

game theory analysis methods to make decisions such as the amount of marketing funds to allocate for a certain product given the potential course of action of potential competitors or the best time to launch a new product, again in light of estimates of opponents' launch plans. To perform a game theory analysis, managers must first determine the players involved, then decide various decision options for each player, before finally assigning the payoff for each envisioned outcome.

IX. KEY PERFORMANCE INDICATORS FOR MANAGERS

Performing a management function is a highly demanding task, which makes it difficult for the individuals involved to keep an eye on the big picture. Managers should therefore attempt to establish a dashboard of relevant KPIs so that they can identify issues early on and assess progress and overall performance.

This dashboard can be maintained through a combination of feedback processes from various entities within the firm as well as a regular analysis task to be assigned to one or more individuals. Not all KPIs need to be quantitative metrics as qualitative assessments can also provide valuable insights at certain times. The KPIs proposed below fall within the following categories:

- Profits:
  - Total revenues.
  - Return by customer.
  - Revenue from customer over time.
  - Sales to expense ratio.
  - Sales margins and profitability.
  - Fixed costs.
  - Variable costs.

- Customers:
  - Customer acquisition rate.

- o Customer retention rate through repeat sales.
- o Customer defection rate.
- o Customer referrals (e.g., using the Net Promotion Score).
- o Customer complaints.
- o Cost to customer.
- o Perceived product or service quality.

- Products or services:
  - o Cost.
  - o Quality.
  - o Dependability of delivery (deliver output to customer on due date).
  - o Speed of delivery.
  - o Flexibility of delivery.

- Innovation:
  - o Percentage of sales versus dates at which underlying ideas were coined. The age distribution of currently commercialized products can indicate the firm's creativity level.
  - o Average time to market an innovation.
  - o Percentage of budget spent on R&D.
  - o Number of patent applications versus time.

- Marketing:
  - o Marketing campaign effectiveness.
  - o Brand equity evaluation.
  - o Conversion rates (e.g., store or website visits versus new customers).
  - o Reputation and sharing on online social networks.

- Suppliers:
  - o Profitability.

- o Prospect.
- o Learning and information exchange.
- o Impact of relationship on firm's image.
- o Honesty/trust.
- o Collaboration.

- Operations:
  - o Staff turnaround times.
  - o Inventory size.
  - o Capacity.

- Employees:
  - o Income.
  - o Well-being (stress).
  - o Work/life balance.
  - o Perceived fairness of treatment.
  - o Shareholders and lenders.
  - o Profitability.

- The market:
  - o Market size.
  - o Market growth.
  - o The firm's market share[267].
  - o Competitors' growth and market shares.

- The firm's financial performance:
  - o Stock price.
  - o Accounting financial indicators (quick ratio, D/E, stock turnover, etc.).

- The economy:
  - o GDP.

---

[267] E.g., a growth in market size without a growth in a firm's share should trigger an alert.

- o Investment levels of the private sector and government expenditure amounts.
- o Household consumption (i.e., expenditure levels).
- o Inflation, which impacts variations in the price of goods.
- o Unemployment figures and wage levels, which reflect the buying power of consumers.
- o International trade.

- Society and the environment:
  - o Legal and regulatory compliance.
  - o Environmental issues.
  - o Other ethical issues.

MBA RELATED ABBREVIATIONS

AIDA	Attention, Interest, Desire, Action
BATNA	Best alternative to a negotiated agreement
BCG	Boston Consulting Group
BCR	Benefits cost ratio
CAGR	Compounded annual growth rate
CAPM	Capital asset pricing model
CCI	Consumer confidence index
CDF	Cumulative distribution function
CLT	Central limit theorem
COGS	Cost of goods sold
COQ	Cost of quality
CPI	Consumer price index
CRM	Customer relationship management
CSA	Country specific advantages
CSR	Corporate social responsibility
DCF	Discounted cash flow
D/E	Debt to equity ratio
DMAIC	Define, measure, analyze, improve, control
EBIT	Earnings before interest and taxes
EBT	Earnings before tax
EBITDA	Earnings before interest, taxes, depreciations, and amortization
EPS	Earnings per share
FCF	Future cash flow
FDI	Foreign direct investment
FIFO	First in, first out
FMA	First mover advantage
FMCG	Fast moving consumer goods
FV	Future value
GDP	Gross domestic product
GNP	Gross national product
HR	Human resources
IMF	International Monetary Fund

IPO	Initial public offering
IRR	Internal rate of return
ISO	International standards organization
IT	Information technology
JIT	Just in time
KPD	Key performance driver
KPI	Key performance indicator
LCL	Lower control limit
LIFO	Last in, first out
M&A	Mergers and acquisitions
MBA	Master in Business Administration
MC	Marginal cost
MNE	Multinational enterprises
MR	Marginal revenue
NGO	Non-government organization
NPS	Net promotion score
NPV	Net present value
PE or P/E	Price to earnings ratio
PEST	Political, economic, social, and technological (analysis)
PESTEL	Political, economic, social, technological, environmental, and legal (analysis)
PLC	Product lifecycle
PPE	Property, plant, and equipment
PV	Present value
R&D	Research and development
RBV	Resource based view
SCM	Supply chain management
SML	Securities market line
SOYD	Sum-of-years-digits
SP	Stock price
SPC	Statistical process control
SWOT	Strengths, weaknesses, opportunities, threats
TPS	Toyota Production System
UCL	Upper control limit

USP	Unique selling proposition
VCA	Value chain analysis
VRIO	Valuable, rare, (hard to) imitate, (exploited by the) organization
WACC	Weighted average cost of capital
WBS	Work breakdown structure
WIP	Work in progress
YTM	Yield to maturity
ZOPA	Zone of potential agreement

BIBLIOGRAPHY

Balzac, Stephen. *The McGraw-Hill 36-hour Course Organizational Development*. New York: McGraw-Hill, 2011. Print.

Barney, Jay B., and Clifford, Trish G. *What I Didn't Learn in Business School: How Strategy Works in the Real World*. Boston, Mass: Harvard Business Review Press, 2010. Print.

Barrow, Colin. *The 30 Day MBA: Your Fast Track Guide to Business Success*. London: Kogan Page, 2011. Kindle edition.

Bensoussan, Babette E., and Fleisher, Craig S. *Analysis without Paralysis: 12 Tools to Make Better Strategic Decisions*. Upper Saddle River, N.J: FT Press, 2013. Kindle edition.

Birkinshaw, Julian M. *Reinventing Management: Smarter Choices for Getting Work Done*. San Francisco: Jossey-Bass, 2010. Print.

Brealey, Richard A., Myers, Stewart C., and Allen, Franklin. *Principles of Corporate Finance*. Boston, Mass.: McGraw-Hill/Irwin, 2008. Print.

Cooper, Cary L., Johnson, Sheena, and Holdsworth, Lynn. *Organisational Behaviour for Dummies*. Chichester: Wiley, 2012. Print.

De Rond, Mark. *There is an I in Team: What Elite Athletes and Coaches Really Know about High Performance*. Boston, Mass: Harvard Business Review Press, 2012. Print.

Edmonds, Thomas P. *Fundamental Financial Accounting Concepts*. Boston, Mass: McGraw-Hill, 2003. Print.

Heskett, James L., Sasser, W E., and Schlesinger, Leonard A. *The Service Profit Chain: How Leading Companies Link Profit and Growth to Loyalty, Satisfaction, and Value*. New York: Free Press, 1997. Print.

Kelley, Tom, and Littman, Jonathan. *The art of Innovation: Lessons in Creativity from IDEO, America's Leading Design Firm*. New York: Currency/Doubleday, 2001. Print.

Kim, W C., and Mauborgne, Renée. *Blue Ocean Strategy: How to Create Uncontested Market Space and Make the Competition Irrelevant*. Boston, Mass: Harvard Business School Press, 2005. Print.

Kotler, Philip, and Keller, Kevin L. *Marketing Management*. Upper Saddle River, N.J: Pearson Prentice Hall, 2009. Print.

Kraus A. and Litzenberger, R.H. "A State-Preference Model of Optimal Financial Leverage." Journal of Finance September (1973): 911-922.

Leseure, Michel. *Key Concepts in Operations Management*. Los Angeles, CA: SAGE, 2010. Print.

Luenberger, David G. *Investment Science*. New York: Oxford University Press, 1998. Print.

Maslow, Abraham H., and Frager, Robert. *Motivation and Personality*. New York: Harper and Row, 1987. Print.

Mason, Joseph B., and Ezell, Hazel F. *Marketing Management*. New York: Macmillan; Toronto: Maxwell Macmillan Canada; New York: Maxwell Macmillan International, 1993. Print.

McGregor, Douglas, and Gershenfeld, Joel. *The Human Side of Enterprise*. New York: McGraw-Hill, 2006. Print.

Mckeown, Max. *The Strategy Book*. Harlow, England; New York: Pearson, 2012. Print.

Meredith, Jack R., Shafer, Scott M., and Turban, Efraim. *Quantitative Business Modeling*. Mason, Ohio: South-Western, 2002. Print.

Mintzberg, Henry. *The Nature of Managerial Work*. Englewood Cliffs, N.J: Prentice-Hall, 1980. Print.

Navarro, Peter. *What the Best MBAs Know: How to Apply the Greatest Ideas Taught in the Best Business Schools*. New York: McGraw-Hill, 2005. Kindle file.

Park, Chan S. *Contemporary Engineering Economics*. Menlo Park, Calif: Addison Wesley, 1997. Print.

Parker, R. H. *Understanding Company Financial Statements*. London: Penguin, 2007. Print.

Patterson, Kerry. *Crucial Confrontations: Tools for Resolving Broken Promises, Violated Expectations, and Bad Behavior*. New York: McGraw-Hill, 2005. Print.

Porter, Michael E. *Competitive Strategy: Techniques for Analyzing Industries and Competitors*. New York, N.Y.: Free Press, 1980. Print.

Porter, Michael E. *Competitive Advantage: Creating and Sustaining Superior Performance*. New York, N.Y.: Free Press Collier Macmillan, 1985. Print.

Porter, Michael E. "How Competitive Forces Shape Strategy." Harvard Business Review 57 (1979): 86-93.

Rahim, M A. *Managing Conflict in Organizations*. Westport, Conn: Quorum Books, 2001. Print.

Robbins, S., and Judge, T. *Organizational Behavior*. Upper Saddle River, N.J: Pearson Prentice Hall, 2009. Print.

Schmenner, Robert W. "How Can Service Businesses Survive and Prosper?" Sloan Management Review, 27.3 (1986): 25.

Silbiger, Steven. *The Ten-Day MBA: A Step-by-Step Guide to Mastering the Skills Taught in America's Top Business Schools*. New York: HarperCollins, 2012. Print.

Slavin, Stephen L. Economics: *A Self-teaching Guide*. New York: Wiley, 1999. Print.

Taleb, Nassim N. *The Black Swan: The Impact of the Highly Improbable*. New York: Random House Trade Paperbacks, 2010. Print.

Thamhain, Hans J. *Management of Technology: Managing Effectively in Technology-intensive Organizations*. Hoboken, N.J: John Wiley, 2005. Print.

Timpere, Adam R. *Corporate Social Responsibility*. New York: Nova Science Publishers, 2008. Print.

Turner, Carol. *A Friendly Introduction to Economics*. Carol Turner, 2012. Kindle edition.

INDEX